easy to make!
Roasts

Good Housekeeping

easy to make!
Roasts

COLLINS & BROWN

This edition published in Great Britain in 2011
by Collins & Brown
10 Southcombe Street
London W14 0RA

An imprint of Anova Books Company Ltd

The Good Housekeeping website is
www.allaboutyou.com/goodhousekeeping

10 9 8 7 6 5 4 3 2 1

ISBN 978-1-84340-650-1

A catalogue record for this book is available from
the British Library.

Reproduction by Dot Gradations Ltd
Printed and bound by Times Offset, Malaysia

This book can be ordered direct from the publisher at
www.anovabooks.com

NOTES

- Both metric and imperial measures are given for the recipes. Follow either set of measures, not a mixture of both, as they are not interchangeable.
- All spoon measures are level.
  1 tsp = 5ml spoon; 1 tbsp = 15ml spoon.
- Ovens and grills must be preheated to the specified temperature.
- Use sea salt and freshly ground black pepper unless otherwise suggested.
- Fresh herbs should be used unless dried herbs are specified in a recipe.
- Medium eggs should be used except where otherwise specified. Free-range eggs are recommended.
- Note that certain recipes, including mayonnaise, lemon curd and some icings and frostings, contain raw or lightly cooked eggs. The young, elderly, pregnant women and anyone with an immune-deficiency disease should avoid these, because of the slight risk of salmonella.
- Calorie, fat and carbohydrate counts per serving are provided for the recipes.
- If you are following a gluten- or dairy-free diet, check the labels on all pre-packaged food goods.
- Recipe serving suggestions do not take gluten- or dairy-free diets into account.

Picture Credits
Photographers: Nicki Dowey (pages 45, 48, 68, 69, 78, 89, 94);
Craig Robertson; Lucinda Symons (pages 24, 28, 76)
Stylist: Helen Trent
Home Economist: Mari Mererid Williams

Contents

Foreword

Cooking, for me, is one of life's great pleasures. Not only is it necessary to fuel your body, but it exercises creativity, skill, social bonding and patience. The science behind the cooking also fascinates me, learning to understand how yeast works, or to grasp why certain flavours marry quite so well (in my mind) is to become a good cook.

I've often encountered people who claim not to be able to cook – they're just not interested or say they simply don't have time. My sister won't mind me saying that she was one of those who sat firmly in the camp of disinterested domestic goddess. But things change, she realised that my mother (an excellent cook) can't always be on hand to prepare steaming home-cooked meals and that she actually wanted to become a mother one day who was able to whip up good food for her own family. All it took was some good cook books (naturally, Good Housekeeping was present and accounted for) and some enthusiasm and sure enough she is now a kitchen wizard, creating such confections that even baffle me.

I've been lucky enough to have had a love for all things culinary since as long as I can remember. Baking rock-like chocolate cakes and misshapen biscuits was a right of passage that I protectively guard. I made my mistakes young, so have lost the fear of cookery mishaps. I think it's these mishaps that scare people, but when you realise that a mistake made once will seldom be repeated, then kitchen domination can start.

This Good Housekeeping Easy to Make! collection is filled with hundreds of tantalising recipes that have been triple tested (at least!) in our dedicated test kitchens. They have been developed to be easily achievable, delicious and guaranteed to work – taking the chance out of cooking.

I hope you enjoy this collection and that it inspires you to get cooking.

Meike.

Meike Beck
Cookery Editor
Good Housekeeping

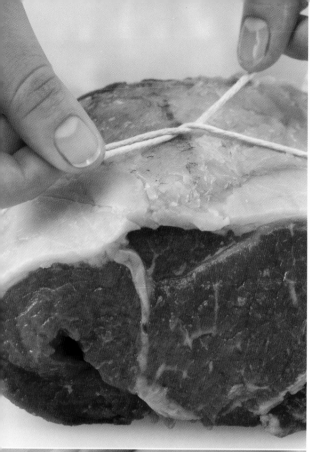

0

The Basics

Chicken and other poultry

Chicken and other poultry such as turkey and duck are perfect for roasting. It's also a simple way to cook young game birds.

Preparing the bird

Take the bird out of the refrigerator 45 minutes–1 hour before roasting to allow it to reach room temperature.

Before stuffing a bird for roasting, clean it thoroughly. Put the bird in the sink and pull out and discard any loose fat with your fingers. Then run cold water through the cavity and dry the bird well using kitchen paper.

Trussing

It is not necessary to truss poultry before roasting it but it gives the bird a neater shape for serving at the table.

1 Cut out the wishbone by pulling back the flap of skin at the neck end and locating the tip of the bone with a small sharp knife. Run the knife along the inside of the bone on both sides, then on the outside. Take care not to cut deep into the breast meat. Use poultry shears or sharp-pointed scissors to snip the tip of the bone from the breastbone, and pull the bone away from the breast. Snip the two ends or pull them out by hand.

2 Pull off any loose fat from the neck or cavity. Put the wing tips under the breast and fold the neck flap on to the back of the bird. Thread a trussing needle and use it to secure the neck flap.

3 Push a metal skewer through both legs, at the joint between thigh and drumstick. Twist some string around both ends of the skewer and pull firmly to tighten.

4 Turn the bird over. Bring the string over the ends of the drumsticks, pull tight and tie to secure the legs.

Poultry and game roasting times

Chicken

To calculate the roasting time for a chicken, weigh the oven-ready bird (including stuffing, if using) and allow 20 minutes per 450g (1lb) plus 20 minutes extra, in an oven preheated to 200°C (180°C fan oven) mark 6.

Oven-ready weight	Serves	Cooking time (approx.)
1.4–1.6 kg (3–3½lb)	4–6	1½ hours
1.8–2.3kg (4–5lb)	6–8	1 hour 50 minutes
2.5–2.7kg (5½–6lb)	8–10	2¼ hours

Turkey

Wrap loosely in a 'tent' of foil, then cook in an oven preheated to 190°C (170°C fan oven) mark 5. Allow 20 minutes per 450g (1lb), plus 20 minutes extra. Remove the foil about 1 hour before the end of cooking time to brown. Baste regularly.

Oven-ready weight	Serves	Cooking time (approx.)
2.3–3.6kg (5–8lb)	6–10	2–3 hours
3.6–5kg (8–11lb)	10–15	3–3¼ hours
5–6.8kg (11–15lb)	15–20	3¼–4 hours
6.8–9kg (15–20lb)	20–30	4–5½ hours

Other poultry

Preheat the oven to 200°C (180°C fan oven) mark 6.

	Serves	Cooking time (approx.)
Poussin	1–2	20 minutes per 450g (1lb)
Guinea fowl		
1.4kg (3lb)	3–4	1½ hours
Duck		
1.8–2.5kg (4–5½lb)	2–4	1½–2 hours
Goose, small		
3.6–5.4kg (8–12lb)	4–7	20 minutes per 450g (1lb)
Goose, medium		
5.4–6.3kg (12–14lb)	8–11	25 minutes per 450g (1lb)

Feathered game

Preheat the oven to 200°C (180°C fan oven) mark 6.

	Serves	Cooking time (approx.)
Grouse	1–2	25–35 minutes
Partridge	2	20–25 minutes
Pheasant	2–4	45–60 minutes

How to tell if poultry is cooked

Test if chicken or turkey is cooked by piercing the thickest part of the meat – usually the thigh - with a skewer. The juices that run out should be golden and clear with no trace of pink; if they're not, return the bird to the oven and check at regular intervals.

Duck and game birds are traditionally served with the meat slightly pink: if overcooked, the meat may be dry.

Resting

Once the bird is cooked, allow it to rest before carving. Lift it out of the roasting tin, put it on a plate and cover loosely with foil and a clean teatowel. Resting allows the juices to settle back into the meat, leaving it moist and easier to carve.

Resting times

Grouse and small game birds	10 minutes
Chicken and duck	15 minutes
Turkey and goose	20–30 minutes

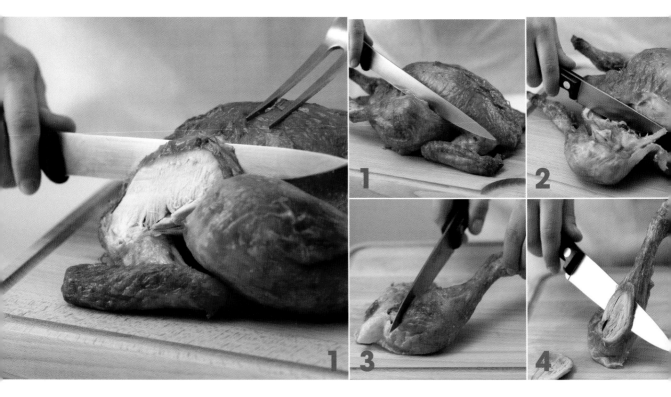

Carving chicken and turkey

After resting, put the bird on a carving board.

1 Steady the bird with a carving fork. To cut breast meat, start at the neck end and cut slices about 5mm (¼in) thick. Use the carving knife and fork to lift them on to a warmed serving plate.

2 To cut off the legs, cut the skin between the thigh and breast.

3 Pull the leg down to expose the joint between the thigh bone and ribcage, and cut through that joint.

4 Cut through the joint between the thigh and drumstick.

5 To carve meat from the leg (for turkeys and very large chickens), remove it from the carcass and joint the two parts of the leg, as above. Holding the drumstick by the thin end, stand it up on the carving board and carve slices roughly parallel with the bone. The thigh can be carved either flat on the board or upright.

Poussins and small game birds

Poussins and other small birds such as grouse can serve one or two people. To serve two, you will need to split them. The easiest way to do this is with poultry shears and using a carving fork to steady the bird. Insert the shears between the legs and cut through the breastbone. As you do this the bird will open out, exposing the backbone; cut through the backbone.

Storing leftovers

Don't forget the leftovers when lunch is finished – never leave poultry standing in a warm room. Cool quickly in a cold place, then cover and chill.

Seasoning

All joints can be seasoned before roasting for extra flavour. Use salt and black pepper. or a dry marinade (see below).

1 Rub the joint with vegetable oil to help the seasonings stick.

2 Press on the seasonings in a thin, uniform layer.

Dry marinades

These don't penetrate far into the meat, but give an excellent flavour on and just under the crust. Make them with crushed garlic, dried herbs or spices, and plenty of freshly ground black pepper. Rub into the meat and marinate in the refrigerator for at least 30 minutes or up to 8 hours.

Roasting know-how

Succulent roasts are simple when you know how. Once the joint is cooked to your liking, make sure it has time to rest before carving to allow the juices to redistribute themselves throughout the meat to give moist, tender results.

Perfect roasting

- Bring the meat to room temperature before cooking – remove from the refrigerator 1–2 hours ahead.
- Cook on a wire rack, or on a bed of sliced vegetables, so that the fat drops away.
- Roast fat side up.
- During cooking, check the juices in the roasting tin to make sure they don't dry up and scorch – this will ruin the gravy. Pour a little freshly boiled water into the roasting tin if necessary.
- When cooked, cover the meat loosely with foil and leave to rest before carving. This makes the meat juicier and easier to carve. Allow meat to rest for at least 15 minutes. A large joint can rest for 45 minutes without getting cold.

1

Pork fillet (tenderloin)

Pork fillet, or tenderloin, can be cooked in a single piece, with or without stuffing. It needs little preparation, but should be trimmed of fat before roasting.

1 Cut off any uneven strips of meat to neaten the shape. Using a sharp small knife, make a cut at the thick end of the tenderloin just underneath the thick, silvery membrane covering it on one side.

2 Taking care not to cut the meat, cut and pull off the membrane in long strips. Make sure every bit of membrane comes away. Trim away any loose scraps of meat, and tidy the ends if they look ragged.

Cooking pork fillet

To cook the fillet unstuffed, heat a little oil in a pan on the hob, add the meat and brown it well on all sides, then finish cooking in an oven preheated to 200°C (180°C fan oven) mark 6 for 20–30 minutes.

To stuff it, make a deep cut along the tenderloin, open it like a book, then pound it gently with a meat mallet or rolling pin to flatten it out. Make a quick stuffing with chopped onion cooked gently in olive oil until soft, then add a little freshly chopped sage or rosemary. Put the stuffing in the centre of the meat, then roll it up and tie with string. Cook the stuffed tenderloin as you would unstuffed, but for 5–10 minutes longer.

Cook's Tip

Test that roast pork is cooked by piercing the thickest part with a skewer. The juices that run out should be clear; if they are pink, return the meat to the oven for 10–15 minutes, then test again.

Pork and ham

Loin of pork produces wonderfully crisp crackling, but many other pork joints are also suitable for roasting, from quick-cooking fillet to pork belly, which requires long, slow roasting for melt-in-the-mouth succulence.

 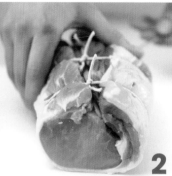

Perfect crackling

- If possible, ask the butcher to score the skin for you.
- The pork skin needs to be dry. Remove the shop's wrapping and pat the skin dry with kitchen paper.
- Leave the joint uncovered in the refrigerator overnight to dry out the skin.
- Use a craft knife or your sharpest knife to score the skin, cutting about halfway into the fat underneath.
- Rub the scored skin with a little olive oil and salt.

Loin of pork

Loin of pork fillet can be cooked on or off the bone. Boned loin of pork may be rolled with or without stuffing, and with or without the skin – which makes the crispy crackling. You can buy boned, rolled and tied pork loin, but if you want to stuff it you will need to tie it yourself.

1 Trim away excess fat and sinews. Shape the stuffing into a thin sheet or cylinder. Lay the loin with the fat side down on the chopping board, and put the stuffing on the line where the eye of loin meets the flap meat. Fold the flap of meat over the eye and secure with skewers.

2 Tie the loin with string every 5cm (2in) and remove the skewers.

Carving pork with crackling

1 It is much easier to slice pork if you first remove the crackling. Remove any string and position the carving knife just under the skin on the topmost side of the joint. Work the knife under the crackling, taking care not to cut into the meat, until you can pull it off with your fingers.

2 Slice the meat, then snap the crackling into servings.

Pork roasting times

Preheat the oven to 180°C (160°C fan oven) mark 4. **Note** Many cooks give pork an initial blast of heat – 220°C (200°C fan oven) mark 7 or even higher – for 15–20 minutes before reducing the temperature. If you do this, watch it carefully near the end of its cooking time.

Off the bone	**Cooking time per 450g (1lb)**
Well done	25-30 minutes
On the bone	**Cooking time per 450g (1lb)**
Well done	30-35 minutes

Use these times as a guideline, but remember that cooking times will vary depending on how the meat has been aged and stored, the shape and thickness of the joint, and personal taste. Ovens vary as well. If a recipe gives a different oven temperature, follow the recipe for timing.

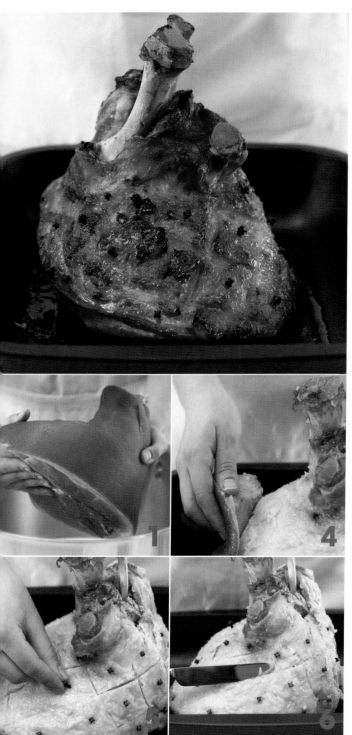

Preparing and cooking ham

Hams come in different sizes and cures. Some are sold cooked, others are uncooked. Some need to be soaked, so buy your ham from a butcher and ask his advice on preparation and cooking.

1 If the ham needs to be soaked, place it in a large container that will hold it comfortably with plenty of space for water. Pour over cold water to cover and weigh down the ham if necessary. Leave to soak overnight, then drain well.

2 Put the ham in a large flameproof casserole, cover with cold water and bring to just below boiling point. Skim off any surface scum. Simmer gently for 25 minutes per 450g (1lb), checking occasionally to make sure it is completely covered with water.

3 Leave to cool in the water. Transfer the ham to a roasting tin. (Reserve the stock for soup.)

4 Preheat the oven to 200°C (180°C fan oven) mark 6. Remove the rind and neatly trim the fat so that there is a 5mm–1cm (¼–½in) layer left on the meat.

5 Score the fat with parallel lines about 5cm (2in) apart, then score on the diagonal to make diamond shapes. Press a clove into the centre of each diamond.

6 Spread prepared English mustard thinly and evenly over the ham – or glaze as the recipe suggests. Sprinkle with soft brown sugar to make a light but even coating. Bake the ham for about 30 minutes, until golden brown.

Cook's Tips

Add a few sprigs of parsley, a few peppercorns, a bay leaf and a chopped onion to the water.
Do not let the water boil at step 2 or the meat will be tough.

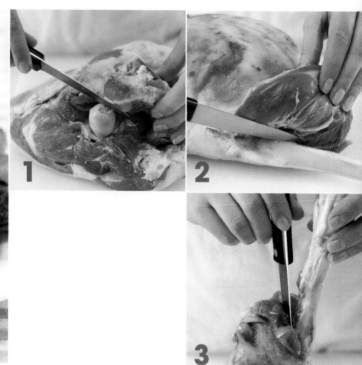

Lamb

Rack of lamb makes a terrific centrepiece for a dinner party, while leg of lamb is a perennially popular Sunday roast.

Butterflying a leg of lamb

Removing the bone makes a tender, easy-to-carve joint.

1 Place the leg of lamb on a board with the meaty side facing down and the bone facing up. With the thick end facing towards you, see if the chunky end of the pelvic bone is in place. If it is, cut it out by working all around it with a boning knife – always cutting towards the bone – then pull or twist it out.

2 Cut a long slit right down to the bone, starting from the thin end, until you reach the joint. Then scrape and cut the meat from the bone, pulling it back with your fingers, until the bone is fully exposed.

3 Work the knife carefully around the bone, cutting away from the meat, to loosen it. Twist out the bone, then follow the same procedure with the other bone.

4 Flatten the meat with your hands. Holding one hand flat on the top of the thickest part, make a cut parallel with the chopping board about midway through. Cut to within 2.5cm (1in) of the edge, then fold the meat out as if opening a book. Repeat with the other thick part of the leg and fold out.

Preparing a rack of lamb

A rack of lamb comprises the seven or eight cutlets – chops from the neck end – served as a joint. Another name for rack of lamb is best end of neck of lamb. Many butchers sell it ready-trimmed, as a French-style rack, but if you need to trim it yourself, here's how.

1 If necessary, pull off the papery outer membrane from the fat side of the rack. Trim away the excess fat. Look for a long strip of cartilage on one end of the rack and cut it out if it is there. Do the same with a long strip of sinew running the length of the rack under the ribs.

2 Make a cut right down to the bone across the fat side of the rack about 2.5–5cm (1–2in) from the tips of the bones. Place the knife in that cut and, holding the knife almost parallel to the ribs, slice off the meat as a single piece to expose the ends of the bones.

3 Insert the knife between one pair of bared ribs at the point of the initial cut. Push through it to cut the meat between the ribs. Continue in the same way with the other ribs.

4 Slice down on both sides of each rib to remove the strips of meat. When you've finished, turn the rack bone side up and scrape off the papery membranes from the backs of the ribs. This will leave the top parts of the bones clean.

Roasting rack of lamb

A rack of lamb should always be cooked at a fairly high temperature so that it browns well without overcooking the eye meat. Preheat the oven to 220°C (200°C fan oven) mark 7 and cook for 25–30 minutes. If you are cooking a single rack, an alternative is to brown the fat side first; this means that you can cook it at a lower temperature, 180°C (160°C fan oven) mark 4.

Carving leg of lamb

There are two ways to carve leg of lamb. The first gives slices with a section of the crust; the second starts with slices that are well done and which then get progressively rarer.

Leg of lamb: method 1

1 Hold the shank and cut from that end, holding the knife flat on the bone, a couple of inches into the meat. Cut down on to the bone to remove that chunk and slice thinly.

2 Start cutting thin slices from the meat on the bone, starting at the cut left by the chunk you removed. Hold the knife at right angles to the bone, then cut at a slight angle as you reach the thicker sections of meat.

3 When you have taken off all the meat you can on that side, turn the leg and continue slicing at an angle until all the meat is removed.

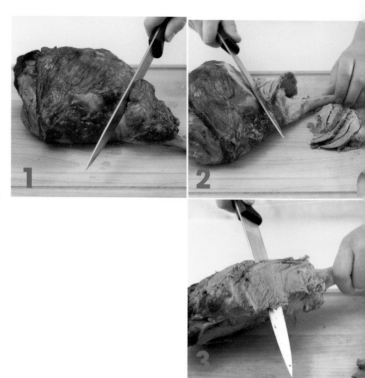

Cook's Tip

To check if roast lamb is cooked as you like it, insert a thin skewer into the centre and press out some juices: the pinker the juice that runs out, the rarer the meat.

Leg of lamb: method 2

1 Hold the shank with the meatiest part of the leg facing up. Slice with the knife blade parallel to the bone. When you reach the bone, turn the leg over and continue slicing (knife blade parallel to the bone) until you reach the bone.

2 Remove the remainder of the meat from both sides in single pieces, and slice thinly.

Lamb roasting times

Preheat the oven to 220°C (200°C fan oven) mark 7. Weigh the joint to calculate the roasting time. Brown the lamb in the hot oven for 20 minutes, then turn the oven down to 190°C (170°C fan oven) mark 5 and roast for the calculated time.

	Cooking time per 450g (1lb)
Medium	15-20 minutes
Well done	20-25 minutes

Use these times as a guideline, but remember that cooking times will vary depending on how the meat has been aged and stored, the shape and thickness of the joint, and personal taste. Ovens vary as well. If a recipe gives a different oven temperature, follow the recipe for timing.

Trimming a joint

1 Cut off the excess fat to leave a thickness of about 5mm (¼in). This isn't necessary for very lean cuts.

2 Trim away any stray pieces of meat or sinew left by the butcher.

3 If the joint has a covering of fat, you can lightly score it – taking care not to cut into the meat – to help the fat drain away during cooking.

Beef

Tender fillet of beef makes a great roast joint that cooks very quickly. Rib, either on the bone or boned and rolled, is a classic choice for roasting. Topside is a good lean joint, but its lack of fat can make it rather dry: it is often sold barded – rolled with a thin layer of fat tied around it to keep it moist during cooking.

Tying

Tie the joint if you are using a boned and rolled joint, or if you have boned the joint but want to roast it using the bones as a 'roasting rack'.

1 Tie a piece of string around the length of the joint, securing it to the bones if you are using them. If you are cooking a boned and rolled joint, turn it 90 degrees then tie another piece in the same way.

2 Starting at one end of the joint, loop string around the meat and tie it securely and firmly. Cut it off and make another loop about 5cm (2in) from the first.

3 Continue tying the joint in this way along the whole length of the joint until neatly and firmly secured.

Larding

Threading narrow strips of fat through lean joints of beef helps to ensure juiciness. The fat is threaded through the joint using a larding needle (available from specialist kitchen stores).

1 Cut long strips of pork fat, preferably back fat, which will fit easily into the larding needle.

2 Push the needle right through the joint, so that the tip sticks out at least 5cm (2in) through the other side.

3 Take a strip of fat, place it in the hollow of the larding needle, and feed it into the tip. When the fat can't go in any further, press down on the joint and pull the needle out. The fat should stay inside.

4 Repeat at 2.5cm (1in) intervals all around the joint.

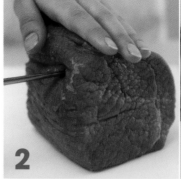

Larding Tips

Larding is much easier if the strips of fat are very cold or even frozen.

The strips of fat don't need to be as long as the joint: you can put several pieces of fat in a single larding channel.

Use one strip per 2.5cm (1in), measuring the longer side of the joint.

Cook's Tip

To check if roast beef is cooked as you like it, insert a thin skewer into the centre and press out some juices. The juices that run out indicate the stage to which the beef is cooked: red juices for rare, pink for medium-rare, or clear for well done.

Beef roasting times

Preheat the oven to 220°C (200°C fan oven) mark 7. Weigh the joint to calculate the roasting time. Brown the beef in the hot oven for 20 minutes, then turn the oven down to 190°C (170°C fan oven) mark 5 and roast for the calculated time.

	Cooking time per 450g (1lb)
Rare	15 minutes
Medium	20 minutes
Well done	25 minutes

Use these times as a guideline, but remember that cooking times will vary depending on how the meat has been aged and stored, the shape and thickness of the joint, and personal taste. Ovens vary as well. If a recipe gives a different oven temperature, follow the recipe for timing.

Stocks

Good stock can make the difference between good gravy and the best gravy. Match the stock to the joint, although chicken stock can be used with pork and vegetable stock works with any meat or poultry. Giblet stock is the traditional basis for gravy for Christmas dinner.

Stocks

Vegetable Stock

For 1.2 litres (2 pints), you will need:
225g (8oz) each onions, celery, leeks and carrots, chopped, 2 bay leaves, a few thyme sprigs, 1 small bunch parsley, 10 black peppercorns, ½ tsp salt.

1 Put all the ingredients in a large pan and add 1.7 litres (3 pints) cold water. Bring slowly to the boil and skim the surface.

2 Partially cover the pan and simmer for 30 minutes. Adjust the seasoning if necessary. Strain the stock through a fine sieve into a bowl and leave to cool.

Meat Stock

For 900ml (1½ pints), you will need:
450g (1lb) each meat bones and stewing meat, 1 onion, 2 celery sticks and 1 large carrot, sliced, 1 bouquet garni (2 bay leaves, a few thyme sprigs and a small bunch parsley), 1 tsp black peppercorns, ½ tsp salt

1 Preheat the oven to 220°C (200°C fan oven) mark 7. Put the meat and bones in a roasting tin and roast for 30–40 minutes, turning now and again, until they are well browned.

2 Put the bones in a large pan with the remaining ingredients and add 2 litres (3½ pints) cold water. Bring slowly to the boil and skim the surface.

3 Partially cover the pan and simmer for 4–5 hours. Adjust the seasoning if necessary. Strain through a muslin-lined sieve into a bowl and cool quickly. Degrease (see opposite) before using.

Chicken Stock

For 1.2 litres (2 pints), you will need:
1.6kg (3½lb) chicken bones, 225g (8oz) each onions and celery, sliced, 150g (5oz) chopped leeks, 1 bouquet garni (2 bay leaves, a few thyme sprigs and a small bunch parsley), 1 tsp black peppercorns, ½ tsp salt.

1 Put all the ingredients in a large pan and add 3 litres (5¼ pints) cold water. Bring slowly to the boil and skim the surface.

2 Partially cover the pan and simmer gently for 2 hours. Adjust the seasoning if necessary.

3 Strain the stock through a muslin-lined sieve into a bowl and cool quickly. Degrease (see right) before using.

Giblet Stock

Use the giblets from a turkey or goose to make stock for gravy. This can be made in advance: cover and chill for up to two days.

To make 1.3 litres (2¼ pints), you will need:
turkey giblets, 1 onion, quartered, 1 carrot, halved, 1 celery stick, halved, 6 black peppercorns, 1 bay leaf.

1 Put all the ingredients in a large pan and add 1.4 litres (2½ pints) cold water. Cover and bring to the boil.

2 Simmer for 30 minutes–1 hour, skimming occasionally. Strain through a sieve into a bowl and cool quickly.

Degreasing stock

Meat and poultry stock needs to be degreased – vegetable stock does not. You can mop the fat from the surface using kitchen paper, but the following methods are easier and more effective. There are three main methods that you can use: ladling, pouring and chilling.

1 **Ladling** While the stock is warm, place a ladle on the surface. Press down and allow the fat floating on the surface to trickle over the edge until the ladle is full. Discard the fat, then repeat until all the fat has been removed.

2 **Pouring** For this you need a degreasing jug or a double-pouring gravy boat, which has the spout at the base of the vessel. When you fill the jug or gravy boat with a fatty liquid, the fat rises. When you pour, the stock comes out while the fat stays behind in the jug.

3 **Chilling** This technique works best with stock made from meat, as the fat solidifies when cold. Put the stock in the refrigerator until the fat becomes solid, then remove the pieces of fat using a slotted spoon.

Cook's Tips

To get a clearer liquid when making meat or poultry stock, strain the cooked stock through four layers of muslin in a sieve.

Stock will keep for three days in the refrigerator. If you want to keep it for a further three days, transfer it to a pan and reboil gently for five minutes. Cool, put in a clean bowl and chill for a further three days.

When making meat or chicken stock, make sure there is a good ratio of meat to bones. The more meat you use, the more flavour the stock will have.

Stuffings

These stuffings are suitable for chicken, turkey or goose. All can be made a day ahead and chilled overnight. Alternatively – with the exception of the wild rice stuffing – all can be frozen for up to one month. Thaw overnight in the refrigerator before using to stuff the bird.

Orange, Sage and Thyme Stuffing

To serve eight, you will need:
2 tbsp olive oil, 1 large onion, finely chopped, 2 garlic cloves, crushed, 75g (3oz) fresh white breadcrumbs, 50g (2oz) pinenuts, toasted and chopped, grated zest of 1 orange, plus 2–3 tbsp juice, 2 tbsp each finely chopped fresh thyme and sage, 1 medium egg yolk, beaten, salt and ground black pepper.

1 Heat the oil and fry the onion and garlic gently for 5 minutes until soft but not brown.

2 Put the remaining ingredients in a large bowl. Add the onion mixture, season and stir to bind, adding more orange juice if needed.

Bacon, Pecan and Wild Rice Stuffing

To serve eight, you will need:
900ml (1½ pints) hot chicken stock, 1 bay leaf and 1 thyme sprig, 225g (8oz) mixed long-grain and wild rice, 50g (2oz) unsalted butter, 225g (8oz) smoked streaky bacon, roughly chopped, 2 onions, finely chopped, 3 celery sticks, finely chopped, ½ Savoy cabbage, chopped, 3 tbsp finely chopped marjoram, 85g sachet sage and onion stuffing mix, 125g (4oz) pecans, chopped.

1 Put the chicken stock in a pan, add the bay leaf and thyme and bring to the boil. Add the rice, cover, reduce the heat and cook according to the packet instructions. Drain if necessary, then tip into a large bowl and cool quickly, discarding the herbs.

2 Melt the butter in a large pan, add the bacon, onions and celery, and cook over a medium heat for 10 minutes until the onions are soft but not brown. Add the cabbage and marjoram and cook for 5 minutes, stirring regularly.

3 Add the cabbage mixture to the rice, together with the stuffing mix and pecans. Tip into a bowl and cool quickly.

Falafel Balls

These stuffing balls are delicious with turkey, but are also great with pitta bread and salad as a vegetarian meal.

To serve eight to ten, you will need:
275g (10oz) dried chickpeas, 1 small onion, roughly chopped, 1 small handful fresh coriander, 3 garlic cloves, roughly chopped, juice of ½ lemon, 2 tsp ground cumin, ½ tsp bicarbonate of soda, olive oil for shallow-frying, salt and ground black pepper.

1 Put the chickpeas in a pan and cover with plenty of cold water. Bring to the boil and boil for 2 minutes, then leave to soak for 2 hours. Drain.

2 Put the drained chickpeas into a food processor with the onion, coriander, garlic, lemon juice, cumin, bicarbonate of soda and ½ tsp salt and pepper. Whiz until everything is finely ground and beginning to stick together. Take small handfuls of the mixture and squeeze in the palm of your hand to extract any excess moisture. Shape into walnut-sized balls.

3 Heat the oil in a frying pan over a medium-high heat and fry the falafel for 3–4 minutes until they turn a deep golden brown all over. Drain well on kitchen paper. Serve immediately, or chill for later use.

4 To use, put the falafel in a parcel of foil and reheat alongside the roast for 15–20 minutes.

Rosemary and Lemon Stuffing

To serve four to six, you will need:
25g (1oz) butter, 1 onion, finely chopped, 125g (4oz) fresh white breadcrumbs, 1 tbsp freshly chopped rosemary leaves, grated zest of 1 lemon, 1 medium egg, beaten, salt and ground black pepper.

1 Melt the butter in a pan, then fry the onion over a low heat for 10–15 minutes or until soft and golden. Tip into a bowl and cool.

2 Add the breadcrumbs, rosemary leaves and lemon zest. Season well, then add the egg and stir to bind.

Pork, Chestnut and Orange Stuffing

To serve eight to ten, you will need:
50g (2oz) butter, 6 shallots, roughly chopped, 4 celery sticks, roughly chopped, 1 fresh rosemary sprig, snipped, 1 tbsp chopped flat-leafed parsley, 175g (6oz) firm white bread, cut into rough dice, 2 cooking apples, about 225g (8oz) total weight, peeled, cored and chopped, 125g (4oz) cooked, peeled (or vacuum-packed) chestnuts, roughly chopped, grated zest of 1 large orange, 450g (1lb) coarse pork sausagemeat, salt and ground black pepper.

1 Melt the butter in a large frying pan and gently fry the shallots, celery and rosemary for 10–12 minutes until the vegetables are soft and golden. Tip into a large bowl. Add the parsley, bread, apples, chestnuts and orange zest to the bowl. Season and mix well.

2 Divide the sausagemeat into walnut-sized pieces. Fry, in batches, until golden and cooked through. Add to the bowl and stir to mix.

Pork, Spinach and Apple Stuffing

To serve eight, you will need:
2 tbsp olive oil, 150g (5oz) onion, finely chopped, 225g (8oz) fresh spinach, torn into pieces if the leaves are large, 2 sharp apples, such as Granny Smith, peeled, cored and cut into chunks, 400g (14oz) pork sausagemeat, coarsely grated, zest of 1 lemon, 1 tbsp chopped thyme, 100g (3½oz) fresh white breadcrumbs, 2 large eggs, beaten, salt and ground black pepper.

1 Heat the oil in a frying pan, add the onion and cook for 10 minutes or until soft. Increase the heat, add the spinach and cook until wilted.

2 Add the apples and cook, stirring, for 2–3 minutes, then set aside to cool. When the mixture is cold, add the sausagemeat, lemon zest, thyme, breadcrumbs and eggs, then season and stir until evenly mixed.

3

4

2

Preparing vegetables

The following frequently used vegetables can be quickly prepared to add flavour to roasts and gravies. Onions and garlic have a pungent taste that becomes milder when they are cooked. Tomatoes and peppers add depth and richness.

Onions

1 Cut off the tip and base of the onion. Peel away all the layers of papery skin and any discoloured layers.

2 Put the onion root end down on the chopping board, then, using a sharp knife, cut the onion in half from tip to base.

3 **Slicing** Put one half on the board, with the cut surface facing down, and slice across the onion.

4 **Chopping** Slice the halved onions from the root end to the top at regular intervals. Next, make two or three horizontal slices through the onion, then slice vertically across the width.

Chillies

1 Cut off the cap and slit open lengthways. Using a spoon, scrape out the seeds and the pith.

2 For finely chopped chilli, cut into thin shreds lengthways, then cut crossways.

Cook's Tip

- -

Wash hands thoroughly after handling chillies – the volatile oils will sting if accidentally rubbed into your eyes.

1   **2**

Garlic

1 Put the clove on a chopping board and place the flat side of a large knife on top of it. Press down firmly on the flat of the blade to crush the clove and break the papery skin.

2 Cut off the base of the clove and slip the garlic out of its skin.

3 **Slicing** Using a rocking motion with the knife tip on the board, slice the garlic as thinly as you need.

4 **Shredding and chopping** Holding the slices together, shred them across the slices. Chop the shreds if you need chopped garlic.

5 **Crushing** After step 2, either use a garlic press or crush with a knife: roughly chop the peeled cloves and put them on the board with a pinch of salt. Press down hard with the edge of a large knife tip (with the blade facing away from you), then drag the blade along the garlic while still pressing hard. Continue to do this, dragging the knife tip over the garlic to make a purée.

Peeling tomatoes

1 Fill a bowl or pan with boiling water. Using a slotted spoon, add the tomato for 15–30 seconds, then remove to a chopping board.

2 Use a small sharp knife to cut out the core in a single cone-shaped piece. Discard the core.

3 Peel off the skin; it should come away easily, depending on ripeness.

Seeding tomatoes

1 Halve the tomato through the core. Use a small sharp knife or a spoon to remove the seeds and juice. Shake off the excess liquid.

2 Chop the tomato as required for your recipe and place in a colander for a minute or two to drain off any excess liquid.

Food storage and hygiene

Storing food properly and preparing it in a hygienic way is important to ensure that food remains as nutritious and flavourful as possible, and to reduce the risk of food poisoning.

Hygiene

When you are preparing food, always follow these important guidelines:

Wash your hands thoroughly before handling food and again between handling different types of food, such as raw and cooked meat and poultry. If you have any cuts or grazes on your hands, be sure to keep them covered with a waterproof plaster.

Wash down worksurfaces regularly with a mild detergent solution or multi-surface cleaner.

Use a dishwasher if available. Otherwise, wear rubber gloves for washing-up, so that the water temperature can be hotter than unprotected hands can bear. Change drying-up cloths and cleaning cloths regularly. Note that leaving dishes to drain is more hygienic than drying them with a teatowel.

Keep raw and cooked foods separate, especially meat, fish and poultry. Wash kitchen utensils in between preparing raw and cooked foods. Never put cooked or ready-to-eat foods directly on to a surface which has just had raw fish, meat or poultry on it.

Keep pets out of the kitchen if possible; or make sure they stay away from worksurfaces. Never allow animals on to worksurfaces.

Shopping

Always choose fresh ingredients in prime condition from stores and markets that have a regular turnover of stock to ensure you buy the freshest produce possible.

Make sure items are within their 'best before' or 'use by' date. (Foods with a longer shelf life have a 'best before' date; more perishable items have a 'use by' date.)

Pack frozen and chilled items in an insulated cool bag at the check-out and put them into the freezer or refrigerator as soon as you get home.

During warm weather in particular, buy perishable foods just before you return home. When packing items at the check-out, sort them according to where you will store them when you get home – the refrigerator, freezer, storecupboard, vegetable rack, fruit bowl, etc. This will make unpacking easier – and quicker.

The storecupboard

Although storecupboard ingredients will generally last a long time, correct storage is important:

Always check packaging for storage advice – even with familiar foods, because storage requirements may change if additives, sugar or salt have been reduced.

Check storecupboard foods for their 'best before' or 'use by' date and do not use them if the date has passed.

Keep all food cupboards scrupulously clean and make sure food containers and packets are properly sealed.

Once opened, treat canned foods as though fresh. Always transfer the contents to a clean container, cover and keep in the refrigerator. Similarly, jars, sauce bottles and cartons should be kept chilled after opening. (Check the label for safe storage times after opening.)

Transfer dry goods such as sugar, rice pasta and flour to moisture-proof containers. When supplies are used up, wash the container well and thoroughly dry before refilling with new supplies.

Store oils in a dark cupboard away from any heat source as heat and light can make them turn rancid and affect their colour. For the same reason, buy olive oil in dark green bottles.

Store vinegars in a cool place; they can turn bad in a warm environment.

Store dried herbs, spices and flavourings in a cool, dark cupboard or in dark jars. Buy in small quantities as their flavour will not last indefinitely.

Refrigerator storage

Fresh food needs to be kept in the cool temperature of the refrigerator to keep it in good condition and discourage the growth of harmful bacteria. Store day-to-day perishable items, such as opened jams and jellies, mayonnaise and bottled sauces, in the refrigerator along with eggs and dairy products, fruit juices, bacon, fresh and cooked meat (on separate shelves), and salads and vegetables (except potatoes, which don't suit being stored in the cold). A refrigerator should be kept at an operating temperature of 4–5°C.

It is worth investing in a refrigerator thermometer to ensure the correct temperature is maintained. To ensure your refrigerator is functioning effectively for safe food storage, follow these guidelines:

To avoid bacterial cross-contamination, store cooked and raw foods on separate shelves, putting cooked foods on the top shelf. Ensure that all items are well wrapped.

Never put hot food into the refrigerator, as this will cause the internal temperature of the refrigerator to rise.

Avoid overfilling the refrigerator, as this restricts the circulation of air and prevents the appliance from working properly.

It can take some time for the refrigerator to return to the correct operating temperature once the door has been opened, so don't leave it open any longer than is necessary.

Clean the refrigerator regularly, using a specially formulated germicidal refrigerator cleaner. Alternatively, use a weak solution of bicarbonate of soda: 1 tbsp to 1 litre (1¾ pints) water.

If your refrigerator doesn't have an automatic defrost facility, defrost regularly.

Maximum refrigerator storage times

For pre-packed foods, always adhere to the 'use by' date on the packet. For other foods the following storage times should apply, providing the food is in prime condition when it goes into the refrigerator and that your refrigerator is in good working order:

Vegetables and Fruit		Raw Meat	
Green vegetables	3–4 days	Bacon	7 days
Salad leaves	2–3 days	Game	2 days
Hard and stone fruit	3–7 days	Joints	3 days
Soft fruit	1–2 days	Minced meat	1 day
		Offal	1 day
		Poultry	2 days
		Raw sliced meat	2 days
		Sausages	3 days

1

Chicken and Poultry

Roast Chicken with Stuffing and Gravy

1.4kg (3lb) chicken

2 garlic cloves

1 onion, cut into wedges

2 tsp sea salt

2 tsp ground black pepper

4 sprigs each fresh parsley and tarragon

2 bay leaves

50g (2oz) butter, cut into cubes

For the stuffing

40g (1½oz) butter

1 small onion, chopped

1 garlic clove, crushed

75g (3oz) fresh white breadcrumbs

finely grated zest and juice of 1 small lemon, halves reserved for the chicken

2 tbsp each freshly chopped flat-leafed parsley and tarragon

1 medium egg yolk

For the gravy

200ml (7fl oz) white wine

1 tbsp Dijon mustard

450ml (¾ pint) hot chicken stock

25g (1oz) butter, mixed with 25g (1oz) plain flour

1 Preheat the oven to 190°C (170°C fan oven) mark 5. To make the stuffing, melt the butter in a pan and fry the onion and garlic for 5–10 minutes until soft. Cool, then add the remaining ingredients, stirring in the egg yolk last. Season well with salt and pepper.

2 Put the chicken on a board breast upwards, then put the garlic, onion, reserved lemon halves and half the salt, pepper and herb sprigs into the cavity.

3 Lift the loose skin at the neck and fill the cavity with stuffing. Turn the bird on to its breast and pull the neck flap over the opening to cover the stuffing. Rest the wing tips across it and truss the chicken (see page 10). Weigh the stuffed bird to calculate the cooking time (see page 11).

4 Put the chicken on a rack in a roasting tin. Season, then add the remaining herbs and the bay leaves. Dot with the butter and roast, basting halfway through, until cooked and the juices run clear when the thickest part of the thigh is pierced with a skewer.

5 Put the chicken on a serving dish and cover with foil. Leave to rest while you make the gravy. Pour off all but about 3 tbsp fat from the tin, put it over a high heat, add the wine and boil for 2 minutes. Add the mustard and stock and bring back to the boil. Gradually whisk in knobs of the butter mixture until smooth; season with salt and pepper. Carve the chicken and serve with the stuffing and gravy.

Serves 5	EASY		NUTRITIONAL INFORMATION
	Preparation Time 30 minutes	**Cooking Time** about 1 hour 20 minutes, plus resting	**Per Serving** 682 calories, 49g fat (of which 21g saturates), 17g carbohydrate, 1g salt

Spicy Roast Chicken with Red Peppers

900g (2lb) floury potatoes, such as Maris Piper, peeled and cut into chunks

2 tbsp sweet paprika

1 tbsp ground coriander

a large pinch of saffron threads, crushed

1 tsp each ground ginger and ground cinnamon

1 head of garlic, plus 2 crushed cloves

juice of ½ orange, plus 1 orange, cut into wedges

2 tbsp olive oil

1.4kg (3lb) chicken

1 small onion, halved

2 red peppers, seeded and cut into eighths

75g (3oz) pinenuts

salt and ground black pepper

1 Preheat the oven to 190°C (170°C fan oven) mark 5. Put the potatoes in a large pan of salted cold water and bring to the boil. Cook for 5 minutes.

2 Meanwhile, put the paprika, coriander, saffron, ginger, cinnamon, 2 garlic cloves, orange juice and oil in a bowl. Add ½ tsp each of salt and pepper and mix well. Put the chicken in a roasting tin and push the orange wedges and onion into the cavity. Season well, then rub the spice mix all over the chicken.

3 Drain the potatoes and shake in a colander to roughen their edges. Put around the chicken. Add the head of garlic and peppers and roast for about 1 hour 20 minutes or until cooked.

4 About 10 minutes before the end of cooking, sprinkle the pinenuts over the chicken. Continue to cook until the juices run clear when the thickest part of the thigh is pierced with a skewer. Carve and serve with the vegetables.

Serves 4	EASY		NUTRITIONAL INFORMATION	
	Preparation Time 30 minutes	**Cooking Time** about 1 hour 25 minutes	**Per Serving** 787 calories, 49g fat (of which 11g saturates), 45g carbohydrate, 0.5g salt	Gluten free Dairy free

900g (2lb) floury potatoes, such as Maris Piper, peeled and cut into chunks

125g (4oz) butter, softened

4 tbsp roughly chopped sage leaves, stalks reserved, plus extra leaves

4 tbsp roughly chopped thyme, stalks reserved, plus extra sprigs

1.4kg (3lb) chicken

juice of 1 lemon, halves reserved

2 fennel bulbs, cut into wedges

1 red onion, cut into wedges

salt and ground black pepper

Mediterranean Roast Chicken

1 Preheat the oven to 190°C (170°C fan oven) mark 5. Put the potatoes in a large pan of salted cold water and bring to the boil. Cook for 5 minutes.

2 Meanwhile, put the butter in a bowl and mix in the chopped sage and thyme. Season well.

3 Put the chicken on a board and push the lemon halves and herb stalks into the cavity. Ease your fingers under the skin of the neck end to separate the breast skin from the flesh, then push the herby butter up under the skin, reserving a little. Season well.

4 Put the chicken in a roasting tin, pour the lemon juice over it, then top with the extra sage and thyme and reserved butter. Drain the potatoes and shake in a colander to roughen their edges. Put around the chicken with the fennel and red onion. Roast for 1 hour 20 minutes or until the juices run clear when the thickest part of the thigh is pierced with a skewer. Carve and serve with the vegetables.

EASY		NUTRITIONAL INFORMATION		Serves
Preparation Time 40 minutes	**Cooking Time** about 1 hour 25 minutes	**Per Serving** 843 calories, 58g fat (of which 26g saturates), 42g carbohydrate, 0.9g salt	Gluten free	**4**

Get Ahead

Complete the recipe to the end of step 2, then chill for up to one day, covered, in a non-metallic dish. Transfer the chicken to a roasting tin before cooking.
To use Complete the recipe.

Chicken in Lemon Vinaigrette

2 lemons

175g (6oz) shallots or onions, sliced

2 tbsp balsamic vinegar

2 tbsp sherry vinegar

4 tbsp clear honey

150ml (5fl oz) olive oil

6 boneless chicken breasts or 12 boneless thighs, with skin

salt and ground black pepper

mashed potatoes to serve

1 Preheat the oven to 200°C (180°C fan oven) mark 6. Grate the zest and squeeze the juice of one lemon, then set aside. Thinly slice the remaining lemon, then scatter the lemon slices and shallots or onions in a small roasting tin – it should be just large enough to hold the chicken comfortably in a single layer.

2 In a bowl, whisk together the lemon zest and juice, vinegars, honey and oil. Put the chicken in the roasting tin, season with salt and pepper and pour the lemon vinaigrette over it.

3 Roast, basting regularly, for 35 minutes or until the chicken is golden and cooked through. Transfer the chicken to a serving dish and keep warm in a low oven. Put the roasting tin, with the juices, over a medium heat on the hob. Bring to the boil and bubble for 2–3 minutes or until syrupy; spoon over the chicken. Serve with mashed potatoes.

Serves 6	EASY		NUTRITIONAL INFORMATION	
	Preparation Time 10 minutes	**Cooking Time** 40 minutes	**Per Serving** 353 calories, 21g fat (of which 4g saturates), 10g carbohydrate, 0.3g salt	Gluten free Dairy free

Stuffed Chicken with Potatoes and Tomatoes

3 large potatoes, peeled and sliced
3 tbsp olive oil
4 chicken breasts with skin
125g (4oz) cream cheese with herbs
300g (11oz) cherry tomatoes on the vine
salt and ground black pepper

1 Preheat the oven to 220°C (200°C fan oven) mark 7. Line a roasting tin with baking parchment and spread the potatoes in the tin. Drizzle with 2 tbsp oil, toss to coat, then roast for 20–25 minutes.

2 Using a sharp knife, ease the skin away from each chicken breast, leaving it attached along one side. Spread the cream cheese across each breast, then smooth the skin back over it. Brush the skin with the remaining oil and season with salt and pepper.

3 Heat a non-stick frying pan over a medium heat until hot, then fry the chicken, skin-side down, for 5 minutes until browned. Carefully turn over, then fry for 5 minutes on the other side.

4 Turn the oven down to 190°C (170°C fan oven) mark 5. Put the chicken on top of the potatoes, add the tomatoes and roast for 10–12 minutes until the chicken is cooked and the juices run clear when the thickest part of the thigh is pierced with a skewer, the potatoes are crisp and the tomatoes roasted.

EASY		NUTRITIONAL INFORMATION		Serves
Preparation Time 10 minutes	**Cooking Time** 30-40 minutes	**Per Serving** 488 calories, 25g fat (of which 11g saturates), 32g carbohydrate, 0.5g salt	Gluten free	**4**

Pesto Roast Chicken

20g (³/₄ oz) fresh basil, roughly chopped
25g (1oz) Parmesan, finely grated
50g (2oz) pinenuts
4 tbsp extra virgin olive oil
1.4kg (3lb) chicken
salt and ground black pepper
roast or new potatoes and green vegetables to serve

1 Preheat the oven to 200°C (180°C fan oven) mark 6. To make the pesto, put the basil, Parmesan, pinenuts and oil in a food processor and mix to a rough paste (if you don't have a food processor, grind in a pestle and mortar). Season with salt and pepper.

2 Put the chicken in a roasting tin. Ease your fingers under the skin of the neck end to separate the breast skin from the flesh, then push about three-quarters of the pesto under the skin, using your hands to spread it evenly. Smear the rest over the chicken legs. Season with pepper and roast for 1 hour 25 minutes or until the chicken is cooked and the juices run clear when the thickest part of the thigh is pierced with a skewer.

3 Put the chicken on a board, cover with foil and leave to rest for 10–15 minutes. Carve and serve with potatoes and green vegetables.

Serves	EASY		NUTRITIONAL INFORMATION	
4	**Preparation Time** 10 minutes	**Cooking Time** about 1 hour 25 minutes, plus resting	**Per Serving** 715 calories, 58g fat (of which 14g saturates), 1g carbohydrate, 0.6g salt	Gluten free

Try Something Different

For a more fiery sauce, add a finely chopped chilli (see page 69) to the devilled mixture before basting.

3 garlic cloves, chopped

1 large onion, chopped

2.3kg (5lb) chicken

450g (1lb) tomatoes, peeled, seeded and chopped

90ml (3fl oz) crème fraîche, warmed, to serve

fresh basil sprigs to garnish

For the devilled sauce

25g (1oz) butter

2 tbsp mango or sweet chutney, any large pieces chopped

2 tbsp Worcestershire sauce

2 tbsp wholegrain mustard

1 tsp paprika

3 tbsp freshly squeezed orange juice

salt and ground black pepper

Chicken with Devilled Sauce

1 Preheat the oven to 190°C (170°C fan oven) mark 5. To make the devilled sauce, melt the butter and mix with the chutney, Worcestershire sauce, mustard, paprika, orange juice, salt and pepper.

2 Put the garlic and onion in the cavity of the chicken. Put the chicken in a roasting tin and spoon over some of the devilled sauce. Roast the chicken, basting frequently with the sauce, for 1³/₄ hours or until the juices run clear when the thickest part of the thigh is pierced with a skewer. The skin should be slightly charred; if it's becoming too brown, cover it with foil towards the end of the cooking time.

3 Put the chicken on a warmed serving plate; keep warm. Skim off the fat from the juices in the roasting tin and discard, then stir the tomatoes into the juices with any remaining devilled sauce. Heat through and season to taste. Carve the chicken and serve with the devilled sauce and warmed crème fraîche. Garnish with basil.

EASY		NUTRITIONAL INFORMATION		Serves
Preparation Time 20 minutes	**Cooking Time** about 1³/₄ hours, plus resting	**Per Serving** 652 calories, 48g fat (of which 17g saturates), 13g carbohydrate, 0.7g salt	Gluten free	**6**

Cook's Tip

To glaze oranges, quarter them or cut into wedges, dust with a little caster sugar and grill until caramelised.

Roast Duck with Orange Sauce

2 large oranges

2 large fresh thyme sprigs

2.3kg (5lb) duck, preferably with giblets

4 tbsp vegetable oil

2 shallots, chopped

1 tsp plain flour

600ml (1 pint) home-made chicken stock

25g (1oz) caster sugar

2 tbsp red wine vinegar

100ml (3½fl oz) fresh orange juice

100ml (3½fl oz) fruity German white wine

2 tbsp orange liqueur, such as Grand Marnier (optional)

1 tbsp lemon juice

salt and ground black pepper

glazed orange wedges (see Cook's Tip) to garnish

mangetouts and broccoli to serve

1 Preheat the oven to 200°C (180°C fan oven) mark 6. Using a zester, remove strips of zest from the oranges. Put half the zest into a pan of cold water, bring to the boil, drain and set aside. Remove the pith from both oranges and cut the flesh into segments.

2 Put the thyme and unblanched orange zest inside the duck; season. Rub the skin with 2 tbsp oil, sprinkle with salt and place, breast-side up, on a rack over a roasting tin. Roast, basting every 20 minutes, for 1¼–1½ hours until just cooked and the juices run clear when the thickest part of the thigh is pierced with a skewer. After 30 minutes, turn breast-side down, then breast-side up for the last 10 minutes.

3 Meanwhile, cut the gizzard, heart and neck into pieces. Heat the remaining 2 tbsp oil in a heavy-based pan, add the giblets and fry until dark brown. Add the chopped shallots and flour; cook for 1 minute. Pour in the stock, bring to the boil and bubble until reduced by half; strain.

4 Put the sugar and vinegar in a heavy-based pan over a low heat until the sugar dissolves. Increase the heat and cook until it forms a dark caramel. Pour in the orange juice and stir. Cool, cover and set aside.

5 Lift the duck off the rack; keep warm. Skim all the fat off the juices to leave about 3 tbsp sediment. Stir the wine into the sediment, bring to the boil and bubble for 5 minutes or until syrupy. Add the stock mixture and orange mixture. Bring back to the boil; bubble until syrupy, skimming if necessary. To serve the sauce, add the blanched orange zest and segments. Add Grand Marnier, if using, and lemon juice to taste.

6 Carve the duck and garnish with mint and glazed orange wedges. Serve with the orange sauce, mangetouts and broccoli.

EASY		NUTRITIONAL INFORMATION		Serves
Preparation Time 50 minutes	**Cooking Time** 1 hour 40 minutes, plus resting	**Per Serving** 561 calories, 38g fat (of which 9g saturates), 20g carbohydrate, 0.5g salt	Dairy free	**4**

Roast Guinea Fowl

1 guinea fowl

2 lemons – grated zest and juice of one, one quartered lengthways

3 bay leaves

5 fresh thyme sprigs

1 tbsp black peppercorns, lightly crushed

25g (1oz) butter

150ml (¼ pint) hot chicken stock

roast potatoes and green beans to serve

For the gravy

2 tbsp redcurrant jelly

100ml (3½fl oz) dry white wine

salt and ground black pepper

1 Put the guinea fowl in a bowl, add the lemon zest and juice, bay leaves, thyme and peppercorns. Cover and leave to marinate for 1 hour. Preheat the oven to 200°C (180°C fan oven) mark 6.

2 Put the bird in a roasting tin, breast-side down, put the lemon quarters and the butter into the cavity, pour the stock over it and roast for 50 minutes.

3 Turn the guinea fowl breast-side up, and continue to roast for 20 minutes or until cooked and the juices run clear when the thigh is pierced with a skewer.

4 Put the guinea fowl on a board, cover with foil and leave to rest for 10 minutes.

5 To make the gravy, put the roasting tin on the hob and scrape up the juices. Add the redcurrant jelly, wine and 50ml (2fl oz) water and bring to the boil. Simmer for 3–5 minutes and season well. Carve the guinea fowl and serve with gravy, roast potatoes and green beans.

Serves 4	EASY		NUTRITIONAL INFORMATION	
	Preparation Time 20 minutes, plus 1 hour marinating	**Cooking Time** 1 hour 10 minutes, plus resting	**Per Serving** 585 calories, 27g fat (of which 11g saturates), 5g carbohydrate, 0.7g salt	Gluten free

Cook's Tip

Use the oil drained from the artichokes to make
a salad dressing.

Poussins with Pancetta, Artichoke and Potato Salad

grated zest of 1 lemon

5 large fresh rosemary sprigs, leaves stripped

4 tbsp white wine vinegar

150ml (¼ pint) fruity white wine

4 garlic cloves, crushed

3 tbsp chopped fresh oregano or a pinch of dried oregano

290g jar marinated artichokes, drained, oil reserved

3 poussins, each weighing about 450g (1lb)

½ tsp cayenne pepper

450g (1lb) new potatoes, quartered

225g (8oz) pancetta or prosciutto or streaky bacon, roughly chopped

350g (12oz) peppery salad leaves, such as watercress, mustard leaf and rocket, washed and dried

salt and ground black pepper

1 Put the lemon zest and rosemary leaves in a large bowl with the vinegar, wine, garlic, oregano and 4 tbsp oil from the artichokes. Stir well. Using a fork, pierce the skin of the poussins in five or six places, then season well with black pepper and the cayenne pepper. Put the birds, breast-side down, in the bowl and spoon the marinade over them. Cover and chill overnight.

2 Boil the potatoes in salted water for 2 minutes. Drain. Preheat the oven to 200°C (180°C fan oven) mark 6.

3 Lift the poussins from the marinade and place, breast-side up, in a large roasting tin. Scatter the potatoes, pancetta and artichokes around them and pour the marinade over. Cook for 1½ hours, basting occasionally, or until golden and cooked through.

4 Cut each poussin in half lengthways; keep warm. Toss the salad leaves with about 5 tbsp warm cooking juices. Arrange the leaves on warmed plates, then top with the potatoes, pancetta, artichokes and poussins.

EASY		NUTRITIONAL INFORMATION		Serves
Preparation Time 20 minutes, plus overnight marinating	**Cooking Time** 1 hour 40 minutes, plus resting	**Per Serving** 442 calories, 27g fat (of which 8g saturates), 13g carbohydrate, 1.5g salt	Gluten free Dairy free	**6**

Cook's Tip

To make parsnip and potato crisps, cut thin strips using a vegetable peeler. Heat a pan half full of sunflower oil until a small cube of bread browns in 20 seconds. Fry the strips, a few at a time, until golden. Drain on kitchen paper and serve immediately.

Roast Grouse

2 oven-ready grouse

6 rashers streaky bacon

2 tbsp vegetable oil

2 tbsp roughly chopped rosemary or thyme (optional)

salt and ground black pepper

deep-fried thinly sliced potatoes and parsnips (see Cook's Tip) or hand-cooked salted crisps and watercress to serve

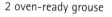

1 Preheat the oven to 200°C (180°C fan oven) mark 6. Put the grouse in a large roasting tin, with enough space between them so that they can brown evenly. Cover the breast of each with rashers of bacon, drizzle with 1 tbsp oil, then season with salt and pepper. Sprinkle with herbs, if using.

2 Roast for about 40 minutes or until the juices run clear when the thigh is pierced with a skewer.

3 Leave to rest in a warm place for 10 minutes before serving.

4 Serve with crisp deep-fried slices of potato and parsnip or ready-made hand-cooked crisps, plus watercress to contrast with the richness of the meat.

Serves	EASY		NUTRITIONAL INFORMATION	
4	Preparation Time 10 minutes	Cooking Time 40 minutes, plus resting	Per Serving 320 calories, 18g fat (of which 4g saturates), trace carbohydrate, 0.3g salt	Gluten free Dairy free

Turkey Crown with Orange

2 onions, sliced

2 bay leaves, plus extra to garnish

2.7kg (6lb) oven-ready turkey crown

40g (1½oz) butter, softened

1 lemon, halved

2 tbsp chicken seasoning

2 oranges, halved

150ml (¼ pint) dry white wine or chicken stock

1 Preheat the oven to 190°C (170°C fan oven) mark 5. Spread the onions in a flameproof roasting tin, add the bay leaves and sit the turkey on top. Spread the butter over the turkey breast, then squeeze the lemon over it. Put the lemon halves in the tin. Sprinkle the chicken seasoning over the turkey and then put the orange halves in the tin, around the turkey.

2 Pour the wine or stock into the roasting tin, with 250ml (9fl oz) hot water. Cover the turkey loosely with a large sheet of foil. Make sure it's completely covered, but with enough space between the foil and the turkey for air to circulate.

3 Roast for 2 hours or until cooked through and the juices run clear when the thickest part of the thigh is pierced with a skewer. Remove the foil and put back in the oven for 30 minutes or until golden.

4 Lift the turkey on to a warmed carving dish, cover loosely with foil and leave to rest for 15 minutes before carving.

EASY		NUTRITIONAL INFORMATION		Serves
Preparation Time 20 minutes	**Cooking Time** 2½ hours, plus resting	**Per Serving** 181 calories, 6g fat (of which 3g saturates), 3g carbohydrate, 0.2g salt	Gluten free	**8**

Spiced Roast Turkey

4.5kg (10lb) oven-ready turkey
Pork, Spinach and Apple Stuffing (see page 25), cooled
2 tsp Cajun spice seasoning
150g (5oz) butter, softened
salt and ground black pepper
herbs to garnish

For the sausages
8 sausages
16 thin rashers streaky bacon

1 Loosen the skin at the neck end of the turkey, ease your fingers up between the skin and the breast and, using a small, sharp knife, remove the wishbone.

2 Preheat the oven 190°C (170°C fan oven) mark 5. Season the inside of the turkey, then spoon the cold stuffing into the neck end only. Neaten the shape, turn the bird over and secure the neck skin with skewers or cocktail sticks. Weigh to calculate the cooking time (see page 11).

3 Put the turkey in a roasting tin, mix the spice with the butter, smear it over the turkey and season. Cover with a tent of foil. Roast for about 3 hours, basting occasionally. If the legs were tied together, loosen after the first hour so that they cook more evenly.

4 Twist each sausage in half and cut to make two mini sausages. Stretch the bacon rashers by running the blunt side of a kitchen knife along each rasher (this stops them shrinking too much when they're cooked). Roll a rasher around each mini sausage. Put in a small roasting tin or around the turkey and cook for about 1 hour. Remove the foil from the turkey 45 minutes before the end of the cooking time.

5 When the turkey is cooked, tip the bird so the juices run into the tin, then put it on a warmed serving plate with the sausages. Cover loosely with foil and leave to rest for 20–30 minutes before carving. Garnish with herbs.

Serves 8	EASY		NUTRITIONAL INFORMATION
	Preparation Time 30 minutes	**Cooking Time** 3 hours, plus resting	**Per Serving** 611 calories, 40g fat (of which 16g saturates), 12g carbohydrate, 2.0g salt

Cook's Tip

When a goose is roasted, a lot of fat is produced: cool, cover and chill for several months. Goose fat makes excellent roast potatoes.

Goose with Roasted Apples

6 small red onions, halved

7 small red eating apples, unpeeled, halved

5kg (11lb) oven-ready goose, washed, dried and seasoned inside and out

1 small bunch fresh sage

1 small bunch fresh rosemary

1 bay leaf

salt and ground black pepper

For the gravy

1 tbsp plain flour

300ml (½ pint) red wine

200ml (7fl oz) Giblet Stock (see page 23)

1 Preheat the oven to 230°C (210°C fan oven) mark 8. Put half an onion and half an apple inside the goose with half the sage and rosemary and the bay leaf. Tie the legs together with string and push a long skewer through the wings to tuck them in. Put the goose, breast-side up, on a rack in a large roasting tin. Prick the breast all over and season with salt and pepper. Put the remaining onions around the bird. Cover with foil and cook for about 3 hours.

2 Roast for 30 minutes, then take the goose out of the oven and baste with the fat that has run off. Remove and reserve any excess fat. Turn the oven down to 190°C (170°C fan oven) mark 5.

3 Put the goose back in the oven and roast for a further 1½ hours, removing any excess fat every 20–30 minutes. Remove the foil. Remove excess fat, then add the remaining apples. Sprinkle the goose with the remaining herbs and roast for a further 1 hour. Transfer to a warmed serving plate, cover with foil and leave to rest for 30 minutes. Remove the apples and onions and keep warm.

4 To make the gravy, pour out all but 1 tbsp of the fat from the tin, stir in the flour then add the red wine and stock. Bring to the boil and cook, stirring all the time, for 5 minutes. Carve the goose, cut the roast apples into wedges and serve with the goose, onions and gravy.

EASY		NUTRITIONAL INFORMATION		Serves
Preparation Time 30 minutes	**Cooking Time** 4¼ hours, plus resting	**Per Serving** 646 calories, 41g fat (of which 12g saturates), 11g carbohydrate, 1g salt	Dairy free	**8**

2

Pork

Honey Pork with Roast Potatoes and Apples

1kg (2¼lb) loin of pork, with crackling and four bones

4 tbsp olive oil

25g (1oz) butter

700g (1½lb) Charlotte potatoes, scrubbed and halved

1 large onion, cut into eight wedges

1 tbsp clear honey mixed with 1 tbsp wholegrain mustard

2 Cox apples, cored and each cut into six wedges

12 fresh sage leaves

175ml (6fl oz) dry cider

salt and ground black pepper

1 Preheat the oven to 240°C (220°C fan oven) mark 9. Put the pork on a board and use a paring knife to score the skin into thin strips, cutting about halfway into the fat underneath. Rub 1 tsp salt and 2 tbsp oil over the skin and season well with pepper. Put the meat on a rack, skin-side up, over a large roasting tin (or just put the pork in the tin). Roast for 25 minutes. Turn the oven down to 190°C (170°C fan oven) mark 5 and continue to roast for 15 minutes.

2 Add the remaining oil and the butter to the roasting tin. Scatter the potatoes and onion around the meat, season and continue to roast for 45 minutes.

3 Brush the meat with the honey and mustard mixture. Add the apples and sage leaves to the tin and roast for a further 15 minutes or until the pork is cooked.

4 Remove the pork from the tin and wrap completely with foil, then leave to rest for 10 minutes. Put the potatoes, onions and apples in a warmed serving dish and put back in the oven to keep warm.

5 Put the roasting tin on the hob, add the cider and stir well to make a thin gravy. Season.

6 Cut the meat away from the bone. Cut between each bone. Pull the crackling away from the meat and cut into strips. Carve the joint, giving each person some crackling, and a bone to chew. Serve with the gravy and potatoes, onion and apples.

EASY		NUTRITIONAL INFORMATION		Serves
Preparation Time 20 minutes	**Cooking Time** 1 hour 40 minutes, plus resting	**Per Serving** 830 calories, 55g fat (of which 19g saturates), 40g carbohydrate, 0.4g salt	Gluten free	**4**

Get Ahead

Complete the recipe up to the end of step 2, cover and chill for up to 24 hours.
To use Complete the recipe.

Pork with Apple and Cream Sauce

25g (1oz) butter

2 large onions, finely sliced

2 tbsp white wine vinegar

1 tbsp demerara sugar

a few fresh rosemary sprigs, chopped

3 red-skinned apples, cored and cut into wedges

2 x 350g (12oz) pork fillets (tenderloin), trimmed

8 slices prosciutto

150ml (¼ pint) double cream

broccoli to serve

1 Preheat the oven to 220°C (200°C fan oven) mark 7. Melt the butter in a frying pan, add the onions and fry for 10 minutes or until softened and golden.

2 Take the pan off the heat and stir in the vinegar, sugar, rosemary and apples. Spoon the mixture over the base of a roasting tin large enough to hold the pork fillets side by side.

3 Wrap the pork in prosciutto, then put on top of the apple mixture. Roast for 30–35 minutes until cooked. Remove the pork and keep warm.

4 Pour the cream into the apple mixture and put back in the oven for 5 minutes. Slice the pork and serve with a little of the creamy apple sauce and some broccoli.

Serves	EASY		NUTRITIONAL INFORMATION	
6	**Preparation Time** 20 minutes	**Cooking Time** 45–50 minutes, plus resting	**Per Serving** 406 calories, 26g fat (of which 13g saturates), 14g carbohydrate, 0.1g salt	Gluten free

700g (1½lb) pork fillet (tenderloin), trimmed

4 tbsp light soy sauce

150ml (5fl oz) red wine

4 tbsp dry sherry

1 tbsp clear honey

1 fresh thyme sprig or a pinch of dried thyme

75g (3oz) dried apricots

100ml (3½fl oz) dry white wine

2 tbsp olive oil

175g (6oz) onions, sliced

2 tsp cornflour

ground black pepper

green vegetables to serve

Pork Fillet with Apricots

1 Put the pork in a non-metallic dish. Combine the soy sauce, red wine, sherry, honey and thyme, season with pepper and spoon over the pork. Cover with clingfilm and marinate in the refrigerator for at least 2 hours or overnight.

2 Meanwhile, put the apricots and white wine in a pan. Bring to the boil, cover and simmer for 20 minutes or until the apricots are soft. Strain, reserving the liquid, and chop the apricots roughly.

3 Preheat the oven to 200°C (180°C fan oven) mark 6. Lift the pork from the marinade; reserve the marinade. Heat 1 tbsp oil in a casserole, add the meat and brown over a high heat. Roast in the oven for 20 minutes or until cooked.

4 Meanwhile, heat 1 tbsp oil in a pan. Add the onions and cook, stirring, for 10–12 minutes until softened. Add the apricots. Keep warm.

5 When the meat is cooked, remove from the casserole and keep warm. Add the marinade and the reserved liquid from the apricots to the juices in the casserole. Blend the cornflour with 1 tbsp cold water and stir into the sauce. Bring to the boil and cook over a medium heat, stirring, for 2 minutes until the sauce thickens.

6 Cut the pork into slices about 1cm (½ in) thick. To serve, spoon a little apricot and onion mixture on to four warmed plates. Put the sliced pork on top and pour a little sauce over it. Serve with green vegetables.

EASY		NUTRITIONAL INFORMATION		Serves
Preparation Time 10 minutes, plus marinating	**Cooking Time** about 20 minutes, plus resting	**Per Serving** 387 calories, 13g fat (of which 3g saturates), 16g carbohydrate, 0.3g salt	Dairy free	**4**

Cider-roast Pork

1.1kg (2½lb) boned rolled loin of pork, fat removed

1 tbsp olive oil

2 red onions, quartered

2 apples, cored and quartered

a few fresh thyme sprigs, chopped

440ml can dry cider

salt and ground black pepper

cabbage to serve

1 Put the pork in a bowl, then add the oil, onions, apples and thyme. Pour in the cider, cover and marinate in the refrigerator for 4 hours or overnight.

2 Preheat the oven to 200°C (180°C fan oven) mark 6. Put the pork in a roasting tin with the marinade ingredients, season, then roast for about 1½ hours or until the pork is cooked. Remove the pork from the roasting tin and leave to rest.

3 To make the cider gravy, drain the roasting juices into a pan, bring to the boil and bubble for 5 minutes until reduced. Slice the pork and serve with the gravy and cabbage.

Serves	EASY		NUTRITIONAL INFORMATION	
4	**Preparation Time** 10 minutes, plus at least 4 hours marinating	**Cooking Time** about 1½ hours, plus resting	**Per Serving** 772 calories, 31g fat (of which 11g saturates), 13g carbohydrate, 0.5g salt	Gluten free Dairy free

Crisp Roast Pork with Apple Sauce

1.6kg (3½lb) boned rolled loin of pork

olive oil

1kg (2¼lb) cooking apples, cored and roughly chopped

1–2 tbsp granulated sugar

1 tbsp plain flour

600ml (1 pint) chicken stock or dry cider

salt and ground black pepper

1 Score the pork skin, sprinkle generously with salt and leave at room temperature for 1–2 hours.

2 Preheat the oven to 220°C (200°C fan oven) mark 7. Wipe the salt off the skin, rub with oil and sprinkle again with salt. Put half the apples in a small roasting tin, sit the pork on top and roast for 30 minutes. Turn the oven down to 190°C (170°C fan oven) mark 5 and roast for a further 1½ hours or until cooked.

3 Meanwhile, put the remaining apples in a pan with the sugar and 2 tbsp water, cover with a tight-fitting lid and cook until just soft. Put to one side.

4 Remove the pork from the tin and leave to rest. Skim off most of the fat, leaving about 1 tbsp and the apples in the tin. Stir in the flour until smooth, stir in the stock and bring to the boil. Bubble gently for 2–3 minutes, skimming if necessary. Strain the sauce through a sieve into a jug, pushing through as much of the apple as possible. Slice the pork and serve with the sauce, roast potatoes and green vegetables.

EASY		NUTRITIONAL INFORMATION		Serves
Preparation Time 30 minutes, plus 1–2 hours standing	**Cooking Time** 2 hours, plus resting	**Per Serving** 769 calories, 50g fat (of which 18g saturates), 22g carbohydrate, 0.4g salt	Dairy free	**6**

Belly of Pork with Cider and Rosemary

2kg (4½lb) piece pork belly roast, on the bone

500ml bottle medium cider

600ml (1 pint) hot chicken stock

6–8 fresh rosemary sprigs

3 fat garlic cloves, halved

2 tbsp olive oil

grated zest and juice of 1 large orange and 1 lemon

3 tbsp light muscovado sugar

25g (1oz) softened butter, mixed with 1 tbsp plain flour

salt and ground black pepper

mixed vegetables to serve

1 Preheat the oven to 150°C (130°C fan oven) mark 2. Put the pork, skin-side up, in a roasting tin just large enough to hold it. Add the cider, stock and half the rosemary. Bring to the boil on the hob, then cover with foil and cook in the oven for 4 hours. Leave to cool in the cooking liquid.

2 Strip the leaves from the remaining rosemary and chop. Put into a pestle and mortar with the garlic, oil, orange and lemon zest, 1 tsp salt and 1 tbsp sugar. Pound for 3–4 minutes to make a rough paste.

3 Remove the pork from the tin (keep the cooking liquid) and slice off the rind from the top layer of fat. Set aside. Score the fat into a diamond pattern and rub in the rosemary paste. Cover loosely with clingfilm and chill until required.

4 Pat the rind dry with kitchen paper and put it (fat-side up) on a foil-lined baking sheet. Cook under a hot grill, about 10cm (4in) away from the heat, for 5 minutes. Turn over, sprinkle lightly with salt, then grill for 7–10 minutes until crisp. Cool, then cut the crackling into rough pieces.

5 Make the gravy. Strain the cooking liquid into a pan. Add the orange and lemon juice and the remaining 2 tbsp sugar, bring to the boil and bubble until reduced by half. Whisk the butter mixture into the liquid and boil for 4–5 minutes until thickened. Set aside.

6 When almost ready to serve, preheat the oven to 220°C (200°C fan oven) mark 7. Cook the pork, uncovered, in a roasting tin for 20 minutes until piping hot. Wrap the crackling in foil and warm in the oven for the last 5 minutes of the cooking time. Heat the gravy on the hob. Carve the pork into slices and serve with the crackling, gravy and vegetables.

EASY		NUTRITIONAL INFORMATION	Serves
Preparation Time 30 minutes, plus cooling and chilling	**Cooking Time** about 4½ hours	**Per Serving** 694 calories, 52g fat (of which 19g saturates), 9g carbohydrate, 0.5g salt	**8**

Fennel-roast Pork

1.6kg (3½lb) loin of pork, boned

4 fresh rosemary sprigs

6 large garlic cloves

3 tsp fennel seeds

300ml (½ pint) dry white wine

salt and ground black pepper

mashed potatoes and curly kale to serve

1 Preheat the oven to 220°C (200°C fan oven) mark 7. Set aside two rosemary sprigs, then strip the leaves off the remainder. Put the garlic, rosemary leaves, fennel seeds, 1 tsp salt and 1 tsp pepper into a food processor and mix to a smooth paste.

2 Score the fat side of the pork with a sharp knife, then rub the flesh side with the garlic and rosemary paste. Rub salt over the fat side. Roll up the loin, then tie along its length at 2.5cm (1in) intervals with fine string. Weigh the meat and calculate the cooking time, allowing 25 minutes per 450g (1lb).

3 Heat a roasting tin on the hob and brown the pork all over, then add the wine and remaining rosemary sprigs. Put in the oven and roast for 20 minutes, then turn the oven down to 200°C (180°C fan oven) mark 6 and roast for the remaining calculated time.

4 Cover the meat with foil and leave to rest for 15 minutes. Slice and serve with the pan juices poured over, with mashed potatoes and curly kale.

Serves	EASY		NUTRITIONAL INFORMATION	
6	**Preparation Time** 25 minutes	**Cooking Time** about 1½ hours, plus resting	**Per Serving** 585 calories, 42g fat (of which 15g saturates), 3g carbohydrate, 0.3g salt	Gluten free Dairy free

175g (6oz) ready-to-eat dried peaches or apricots
400ml (14fl oz) unsweetened apple juice
grated zest and juice of 1 small orange
175ml (6fl oz) extra virgin olive oil
3 tbsp freshly chopped flat-leafed parsley
1 tbsp freshly chopped chives
1.8kg (4lb) loin of pork, boned
1.1kg (2½lb) potatoes
6-8 fresh rosemary sprigs, leaves stripped
1 tbsp plain flour
salt and ground black pepper
carrots to serve

Roast Pork with Peaches

1 Soak the dried peaches or apricots in half the apple juice overnight.

2 Drain the fruit (keep the juice) and put in a food processor; chop roughly. Add the orange zest, 4 tbsp oil and the herbs and mix together; season with salt and pepper.

3 If the pork has crackling, remove it carefully with a sharp knife, lay it in a small roasting tin, rub lightly with 1 tbsp oil and sprinkle with salt. Set aside.

4 Place the pork, fat-side up, on a board, then split it almost in half by slicing horizontally through the eye of the meat towards the fatty side. Open it like a book, spread the fruit stuffing on the bottom half and reshape. Tie with string; set aside.

5 Preheat the oven to 200°C (180°C fan oven) mark 6. Cut the potatoes into wedges and boil for 1-2 minutes; drain, reserving the water. Return the potatoes to the pan over a low heat to dry them off.

Toss in the remaining oil and rosemary leaves and season. Put in a roasting tin and roast for 20-30 minutes.

6 Put the pork on a rack over the potatoes and spoon the reserved apple juice over it. Put the crackling on the shelf above the pork. Cook for a further 1¼-1½ hours, basting from time to time, until the pork is cooked and the crackling is crisp. Put the pork, crackling and potatoes on a serving plate and keep warm.

7 Add the flour to the juices in the roasting tin. Put the tin on the hob and stir for 1-2 minutes over a medium heat until smooth. Pour in the orange juice, remaining apple juice and potato water, then bring to the boil and simmer for 3-4 minutes until slightly thickened.

8 Slice the pork and crackling, strain the gravy and serve with the pork, potatoes and carrots.

EASY		NUTRITIONAL INFORMATION		Serves
Preparation Time 1 hour, plus overnight soaking	**Cooking Time** 1 hour 50 minutes, plus resting	**Per Serving** 617 calories, 40g fat (of which 12g saturates), 37g carbohydrate, 0.2g salt	Dairy free	**8**

Cook's Tips

You will need a pressure cooker for this recipe.
Instead of discarding the stock at step 2, chill or freeze; use to make soup.

Quick Roast Ham

1kg (2¼lb) unsmoked boneless gammon joint

6 whole allspice berries

2–3 sprigs each fresh thyme and parsley

6 black peppercorns

225g (8oz) each baby carrots and baby leeks

225g (8oz) baby parsnips, halved

225g (8oz) shallots, halved if large

2 small green cabbages, total weight about 450g (1lb), quartered

3 tbsp wholegrain mustard

3 tbsp clear honey

3 tbsp olive oil

salt and ground black pepper

1 Put the gammon in a pressure cooker. Pour in enough water to half-fill the pan, then add the allspice, thyme, parsley and peppercorns. Cover, put to the highest setting and bring up to pressure. Following the manufacturer's instructions, cook for 25 minutes. If your pressure cooker doesn't have a steam quick-release system, run the cold tap in the sink and hold the pan underneath it to reduce the pressure quickly. Lift out the gammon, then cover and put to one side.

2 Bring the stock back to the boil. Add the carrots, leeks, parsnips, shallots and cabbages and blanch for 2 minutes. Drain well, discarding the stock.

3 Preheat the oven to 240°C (220°C fan oven) mark 9. Put the ham in a roasting tin along with the blanched vegetables. Mix together the mustard, honey and 1 tbsp oil and drizzle over the ham. Pour the rest of the oil over the vegetables and season. Roast for 10–15 minutes until golden. Slice the ham and serve hot, with the vegetables.

Serves	EASY		NUTRITIONAL INFORMATION	
4	**Preparation Time** 20 minutes	**Cooking Time** 35–40 minutes	**Per Serving** 574 calories, 29g fat (of which 8g saturates), 31g carbohydrate, 6g salt	Gluten free Dairy free

Cook's Tip

Home-cooked ham is great hot or cold, but cooking a large joint is often impractical. Roasting two medium joints at the same time means you can serve a hot joint and have plenty left to eat cold.

Maple, Ginger and Soy-roasted Gammon

2 x 2.5kg (5½lb) smoked boneless gammon joints

8 tbsp vegetable oil

7.5cm (3in) piece fresh root ginger, grated

8 tbsp maple syrup

6 tbsp dark soy sauce

12 star anise (optional)

1 If the gammon is salty (check with your butcher), soak it in cold water overnight. Alternatively, bring to the boil in a large pan of water and simmer for 10 minutes.

2 Preheat the oven to 200°C (180°C fan oven) mark 6. Put the joints in a roasting tin and pour 4 tbsp oil over them. Cover with foil and roast for 1 hour 50 minutes or 20 minutes per 450g (1lb).

3 Mix together the ginger, maple syrup, soy sauce and the remaining vegetable oil in a bowl.

4 Take the gammon out of the oven, remove the foil and allow to cool a little, then carefully peel away the skin and discard. Score the fat in a criss-cross pattern, stud with the star anise if using, then pour the ginger sauce over the gammon. Continue to roast for another 20 minutes or until the glaze is golden brown. Slice and serve one joint warm. Cool the other, wrap in foil and chill until needed.

EASY		NUTRITIONAL INFORMATION		Serves
Preparation Time 10 minutes	**Cooking Time** 2 hours 10 minutes	**Per Serving** 392 calories, 21g fat (of which 7g saturates), 2g carbohydrate, 6.1g salt	Dairy free	**18**

Cook's Tip

Ask the butcher to weigh the gammon for you. It will save you struggling to do it at home when you need to calculate the cooking time.

Sugar-baked Gammon

4.5kg (10lb) smoked gammon joint on the bone
1 bay leaf
6 tbsp Dijon mustard
6 tbsp demerara sugar
1 tbsp whole cloves
roasted root vegetables, carrots, green vegetables and wholegrain mustard to serve

1 If the gammon is salty (check with your butcher), soak it with the bay leaf in cold water overnight. Alternatively, bring to the boil in a large pan of water and simmer for 10 minutes.

2 Drain the gammon well and discard the bay leaf. Preheat the oven to 170°C (150°C fan oven) mark 3. Line a large roasting tin with a double layer of foil and put the gammon on top. Cover loosely with a large tent of foil and bake for 3 hours 20 minutes or 20 minutes per 450g (1lb).

3 About 30 minutes before the end of cooking, increase the oven temperature to 220°C (200°C fan oven) mark 7. Drain any juices from the tin. Run a sharp knife just under the rind to remove it, taking care to leave as much of the fat on the gammon as possible. The rind will peel off easily in strips, but you may need to use a cloth as it will be hot.

4 Score a large diamond pattern into the fat on the gammon. Mix together the mustard and sugar, then spread over the fat to cover completely. Stud it here and there with the cloves.

5 Roast uncovered for 30 minutes or until golden. Turn off the oven and leave the gammon inside to rest for 20 minutes before carving. Serve the gammon hot, cut into thick slices with a selection of vegetables and mustard.

Serves	EASY		NUTRITIONAL INFORMATION	
6	Preparation Time 20 minutes, plus soaking	Cooking Time 3 hours 20 minutes, plus resting	Per Serving 345 calories, 19g fat (of which 6g saturates), 0g carbohydrate, 5.5g salt	Gluten free Dairy free

3

Lamb

Try Something Different

Roast Lamb with Lemon and Thyme: use lemon zest and juice instead of orange and replace the rosemary with 3–4 large fresh thyme sprigs.

grated zest and juice of 1 orange, plus extra wedges to garnish

2 garlic cloves, sliced

3 large fresh rosemary sprigs, leaves stripped

1 tbsp olive oil

1.4kg (3lb) leg of lamb

3 tbsp orange marmalade

1 tbsp plain flour

salt and ground black pepper

roasted vegetables to serve

Roast Lamb with Orange

1 Preheat the oven to 180°C (160°C fan oven) mark 4. In a bowl, mix together the orange zest, garlic, the leaves from 2 rosemary sprigs and the oil. Season. Put the lamb on a board and make several slits all over it. Stuff the mixture into the slits. Put the lamb on a rack in a roasting tin and roast for 1¼ hours, basting with the juices from time to time.

2 About 10–15 minutes before the end of the cooking time, brush the lamb with the marmalade. Insert a few rosemary leaves into each slit in the meat.

3 Remove the lamb from the oven, wrap loosely in foil and leave to rest for 10–15 minutes.

4 Put the roasting tin on the hob, skim off and discard the fat and stir in the flour. Add 150ml (¼ pint) water and the orange juice and bring to the boil, then simmer, stirring occasionally, for 8 minutes or until thick. Season. Carve the lamb and serve with the gravy and vegetables; garnish with orange wedges.

Serves	EASY		NUTRITIONAL INFORMATION	
4	**Preparation Time** 20 minutes	**Cooking Time** 1 hour 25 minutes, plus resting	**Per Serving** 581 calories, 28g fat (of which 12g saturates), 14g carbohydrate, 0.4g salt	Dairy free

Cook's Tips

Chillies vary enormously in strength, from quite mild to blisteringly hot, depending on the type of chilli and its ripeness. Taste a small piece first to check it's not too hot for you.

To prepare, see page 26.

Be extremely careful when handling chillies not to touch or rub your eyes with your fingers, as they will sting. Wash knives immediately after handling chillies for the same reason. As a precaution, use rubber gloves when preparing them if you like.

Roast Spiced Leg of Lamb

1.6–1.8kg (3½–4lb) leg of lamb

2 tbsp each cumin seeds and coriander seeds

50g (2oz) blanched or flaked almonds

1 medium onion, chopped

6 garlic cloves, roughly chopped

2.5cm (1in) piece fresh root ginger, grated

4 hot green chillies, seeded and chopped (see Cook's Tips)

500g carton natural yogurt

½ tsp each cayenne pepper and garam masala

3½ tsp salt

4 tbsp vegetable oil

½ tsp whole cloves, 16 cardamom pods, 1 cinnamon stick, 10 black peppercorns

flat-leafed parsley sprigs to garnish

1 Put the lamb into a large shallow ceramic dish and set aside. Put the cumin and coriander seeds in a pan and cook over a high heat until aromatic. Grind to a fine powder in a mortar and pestle. Set aside.

2 Put the almonds, onion, garlic, ginger, chillies and 3 tbsp yogurt in a food processor and blend to a paste. Put the remaining yogurt into a bowl, stir well and add the paste, ground cumin and coriander, cayenne pepper, garam masala and salt. Stir well.

3 Spoon the yogurt mixture over the lamb and use a brush to push it into all the nooks and crannies. Turn the lamb, making sure it is well coated, then cover and leave to marinate in the refrigerator for 24 hours.

4 Preheat the oven to 200°C (180°C fan oven) mark 6. Put the lamb and marinade in a roasting tin. Heat the oil in a small frying pan, add the cloves, cardamom pods, cinnamon and peppercorns, and fry until they begin to release their aromas. Pour over the lamb. Cover the roasting tin with foil and roast for 1½ hours. Remove the foil and roast for a further 45 minutes, basting occasionally. Put the lamb on a serving dish; pick out the spices to garnish. Press the sauce through a fine sieve into a bowl. Garnish the lamb with parsley and serve the sauce on the side.

EASY		NUTRITIONAL INFORMATION		Serves
Preparation Time 25 minutes, plus 24 hours marinating	**Cooking Time** 2¼ hours	**Per Serving** 671 calories, 47g fat (of which 13g saturates), 11g carbohydrate, 2.2g salt	Gluten free	**6**

Lamb Boulangère

1.8kg (4lb) waxy potatoes such as King Edward, finely sliced

1 onion, sliced and blanched in boiling water for 2 minutes

600ml (1 pint) vegetable stock

5 garlic cloves, crushed

3 tbsp finely chopped fresh mint

2 tbsp finely chopped fresh rosemary

100g (3½oz) butter, at room temperature, plus extra to grease

1 leg of lamb, weighing around 2.3kg (5lb)

salt and ground black pepper

For the red pepper salsa

3 red peppers

2 tbsp extra virgin olive oil, plus extra to drizzle

1 small red onion, finely sliced

juice of ½ lemon

1–2 tbsp baby capers, rinsed

5 fresh mint leaves, finely chopped

1 Preheat the oven to 200°C (180°C fan oven) mark 6. Butter a 4.5 litre (8 pint) roasting tin. Layer the potatoes and onion, seasoning with salt and pepper as you go. Pour the stock over them and roast for 30 minutes.

2 Put the garlic, herbs and butter in a bowl and mix together. Season well. Put the lamb on a board and trim away any excess fat. Make about six or seven deep cuts all over. Use a teaspoon to push the butter mixture into the cuts, then smear the rest all over the leg. Put on a rack over the potatoes. Roast for 1 hour 40 minutes or 20 minutes per 450g (1lb).

3 Meanwhile, make the red pepper salsa. Put the peppers in a roasting tin, drizzle with a little oil and roast in the oven with the lamb for 30–40 minutes or until the skins are slightly charred. Put in a bowl, cover with clingfilm and leave to cool.

4 Put the red onion in a bowl, add the lemon juice, season with salt and leave to marinate. Peel the peppers, slice the flesh and put in a bowl with any juice. Add the capers, oil and mint. Season well. Stir everything together.

5 Put the lamb on a board, cover with foil and leave to rest for 10 minutes. Leave the potatoes in the oven to keep hot while you carve the lamb. Serve the sliced meat with the potatoes and red pepper salsa.

Serves 6	EASY		NUTRITIONAL INFORMATION	
	Preparation Time 40 minutes	**Cooking Time** about 2¼ hours, plus resting	**Per Serving** 998 calories, 61g fat (of which 24g saturates), 53g carbohydrate, 0.8g salt	Gluten free

Get Ahead

Make the harissa, spoon into a screw-topped jar, cover with olive oil and chill for up to one week.
Prepare the lamb as in step 2, cover and chill for up to one day.
To use Take lamb out of the refrigerator 30 minutes before completing the recipe.

Roast Lamb with Harissa

1.8kg (4lb) boned leg of lamb, plus bones

2 tbsp olive oil

1 bunch of rosemary

1 bunch of thyme

350g (12oz) shallots, peeled, root left intact and blanched

1 head of garlic, broken up into cloves, skin left on

300ml (½ pint) dry white wine

600ml (1 pint) lamb or chicken stock

salt and ground black pepper

couscous sprinkled with freshly chopped coriander to serve

grilled chillies to garnish (optional)

For the harissa

2 large red peppers, about 400g (14oz) total weight

4 large fresh red chillies, seeded and roughly chopped (see page 69)

6 garlic cloves

1 tbsp each ground coriander and caraway seeds

2 tsp salt

4 tbsp olive oil

1 To make the harissa, grill the peppers until the skins are completely blackened and the flesh is soft, then cover and leave to cool. Peel off the skins; remove the cores and seeds. Put the chillies in a food processor with the garlic, coriander and caraway seeds and blend to a paste. Add the peppers, salt and oil and blend for 1–2 minutes until smooth.

2 To prepare the lamb, spread the bone cavity with about 3 tbsp harissa. Roll and secure with cocktail sticks or sew up using a trussing needle and thread.

3 Preheat the oven to 200°C (180°C fan oven) mark 6. Heat the oil in a roasting pan on the hob and brown the lamb on all sides. Season, place the rosemary and thyme under the lamb and add the bones to the roasting tin. Roast for 1 hour for pink lamb or 1½ hours for well-done. Baste from time to time and add the shallots and garlic to the roasting pan 45 minutes before the end of the cooking time.

4 Transfer the lamb to a carving plate with the shallots and garlic. Cover loosely with foil and leave to rest in the oven on a low heat.

5 Skim off any fat from the roasting tin and put on the hob. Add the wine, bring to the boil and bubble until reduced by half. Add the stock and bubble until reduced by half. Season, then strain. Remove the cocktail sticks or thread from the lamb and slice. Serve with the shallots, garlic, gravy and couscous. Garnish with chillies if you like.

EASY		NUTRITIONAL INFORMATION		Serves
Preparation Time 40 minutes	**Cooking Time** about 1 hour 40 minutes, plus resting	**Per Serving** 645 calories, 45g fat (of which 13g saturates), 6g carbohydrate, 2g salt	Dairy free	**6**

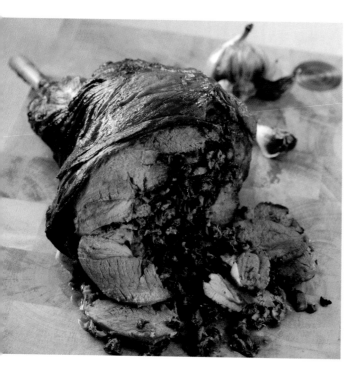

Get Ahead

Make the stuffing, cover and chill for up to one day.

Stuffed Leg of Lamb

1 leg of lamb, about 2.7kg (6lb), knucklebone removed but end bone left in

2 garlic bulbs

Redcurrant Sauce (see page 123) to serve

For the stuffing

25g (1oz) butter

75ml (3fl oz) olive oil

1 small red onion, finely chopped

450g (1lb) chestnut mushrooms, finely chopped

4 tbsp freshly chopped flat-leafed parsley, 1 tbsp freshly chopped oregano and 6–8 thyme sprigs, leaves stripped

salt and ground black pepper

1 First make the stuffing. Melt the butter in a frying pan with 2 tbsp oil. Fry the onion gently for 10–15 minutes until soft. Add the mushrooms and cook for 15–20 minutes – the mixture will become dryish – stirring all the time, until the mushrooms begin to turn golden brown. Add the herbs and cook for 1 minute. Season and leave to cool.

2 Preheat the oven to 190°C (170°C fan oven) mark 5. Open out the lamb and spread the stuffing over the meat. Reshape the lamb and secure with string. Put the lamb in a roasting tin and season. Roast, basting occasionally, for 2½–3 hours.

3 About 1 hour before the end of the cooking time, rub the whole garlic bulbs with the remaining oil and put them alongside the lamb until very soft.

4 When the lamb is cooked to your liking, transfer to a carving board, cover with a tent of foil and leave to rest. Keep the garlic warm until ready to serve.

5 Carve the lamb and garnish with the roasted garlic, broken into cloves. Serve with Redcurrant Sauce.

Serves	EASY		NUTRITIONAL INFORMATION	
8	**Preparation Time** 40 minutes	**Cooking Time** 3 hours–3 hours 40 minutes, plus resting	**Per Serving** 632 calories, 47g fat (of which 15g saturates), 1g carbohydrate, 0.4g salt	Gluten free

Cook's Tip

Butterflied lamb is a leg of lamb with the bone removed (see page 17). Most butchers will do this for you.

Garlic, Lemon and Thyme Butterflied Lamb

1 leg of lamb, about 2.3kg (5lb), boned

175ml (6fl oz) extra virgin olive oil, plus extra to brush

1 tbsp dried oregano

3 tbsp fresh thyme leaves

2 tbsp freshly chopped flat-leafed parsley

6 garlic cloves, finely chopped

150ml (5fl oz) balsamic vinegar

grated zest and juice of 2 small lemons

roast potatoes and green vegetables or cherry tomatoes and mixed leaf salad to serve

1 Open out the meat, lay skin-side down and trim away any excess fat. Make slits all over it to help the marinade penetrate the flesh. Put the lamb in a ceramic dish large enough to hold it in a single layer. Whisk the oil, herbs, garlic, vinegar, lemon zest and juice together in a small bowl and pour over the meat, rubbing well into the slits. Cover and leave to marinate overnight in the refrigerator.

2 Remove from the refrigerator an hour before cooking. Preheat the oven to 220°C (200°C fan oven) mark 7. Lift from the marinade (don't throw it away) and roast for 20 minutes, then turn down the oven to 190°C (170°C fan oven) mark 5 and roast for a further 1 hour 10 minutes, basting with the reserved marinade from time to time, or until the meat is cooked but still slightly pink in the centre.

3 Put the lamb on a board and cover loosely with foil. Leave to rest for 10 minutes before carving. Serve with potatoes and vegetables or salad.

EASY		NUTRITIONAL INFORMATION		Serves
Preparation Time 20 minutes, plus overnight marinating	**Cooking Time** about 1¼ hours, plus resting	**Per Serving** 509 calories, 32g fat (of which 13g saturates), 1g carbohydrate, 0.3g salt	Gluten free Dairy free	**8**

Rack of Lamb with Balsamic Gravy

4 fat garlic cloves, crushed

2 tbsp herbes de Provence

6 tbsp balsamic vinegar

12 tbsp olive oil

4 trimmed racks of lamb

salt and ground black pepper

1 Preheat the oven to 220°C (200°C fan oven) mark 7. Put the garlic in a bowl with the herbs, 2 tbsp vinegar and 4 tbsp oil. Season with salt and pepper.

2 Put the lamb in a roasting tin and rub the garlic mixture into both the fat and meat. Roast for 25–30 minutes if you like the meat pink, or cook for a further 5–10 minutes if you like it well done. Lift the lamb on to a warmed serving dish, cover with foil and leave to rest for 10 minutes.

3 Put the roasting tin on the hob over a medium heat and whisk in the remaining vinegar and oil, scraping up any sediment as the liquid bubbles. Pour the gravy into a small jug.

4 Slice the lamb into cutlets and serve with the gravy.

Serves	EASY		NUTRITIONAL INFORMATION	
8	**Preparation Time** 5 minutes	**Cooking Time** 30–45 minutes, plus resting	**Per Serving** 410 calories, 37g fat (of which 14g saturates), 1g carbohydrate, 0.2g salt	Gluten free Dairy free

Rack of Lamb with Rosemary and Red Wine Sauce

2 garlic cloves, crushed

3 trimmed racks of lamb

300ml (½ pint) red wine

6 rosemary sprigs, roughly crushed to release the flavour

1 tbsp olive oil

300g carton fresh lamb stock

3 tbsp redcurrant jelly

knob of herb butter

salt and ground black pepper

green vegetables and potato and carrot mash to serve

1 Rub the garlic into the meat, then put in a shallow, sealable container and add the wine and rosemary. Cover and marinate in the refrigerator for at least 4 hours or overnight.

2 Preheat the oven to 200°C (180°C fan oven) mark 6. Drain off the marinade and put to one side. Pat the meat dry with kitchen paper and put in a roasting tin with the rosemary. Drizzle with oil, season with salt and pepper and roast for 15–20 minutes.

3 Meanwhile, put the marinade in a wide, heavy-based pan, bring to the boil and reduce by half. Add the stock and jelly and bring to the boil, then simmer for 10–12 minutes to reduce to a syrupy sauce.

4 Take the lamb out of the oven and leave to rest for 5–10 minutes. Add the herb butter to the sauce, along with juices from the roasting tin. Whisk in and season to taste. Slice the lamb into cutlets, garnish with rosemary, drizzle with sauce and serve with vegetables and mash.

EASY		NUTRITIONAL INFORMATION		Serves
Preparation Time 10 minutes, plus at least 4 hours marinating	**Cooking Time** 15–20 minutes, plus resting	**Per Serving** 355 calories, 26g fat (of which 12g saturates), 5g carbohydrate, 0.2g salt	Gluten free	**6**

Guard of Honour with Hazelnut and Herb Crust

2 trimmed racks of lamb

salt and ground black pepper

roasted root vegetables to serve

For the hazelnut and herb crust

75g (3oz) fresh breadcrumbs made from Italian bread, such as ciabatta

2 tbsp each chopped fresh flat-leafed parsley and thyme

1 tbsp chopped fresh rosemary

2 garlic cloves, crushed

2 tbsp olive oil

50g (2oz) hazelnuts, toasted and roughly chopped

4 tbsp Dijon mustard

1 Preheat the oven to 200°C (180°C fan oven) mark 6. Trim off as much of the fat from the lamb as possible and set aside. Season the lamb well with pepper.

2 Heat the reserved fat in a large heavy-based frying pan, add the lamb and sear on both sides. Remove the lamb from the pan and set aside until cool enough to handle. Put the racks together so the ribs interlock. Place the lamb in a roasting tin, rib bones uppermost, with the lamb fat. Roast for 10 minutes.

3 Meanwhile, make the hazelnut crust. Combine the breadcrumbs, herbs, garlic, oil and seasoning for 30 seconds in a food processor, then add the hazelnuts and pulse for a further 30 seconds.

4 Remove the lamb from the oven and spread the fatty side with the mustard. Press the hazelnut crust on to the mustard.

5 Baste the lamb with the fat in the roasting tin and put back in the oven for 15–20 minutes for rare, 20–25 minutes for medium-rare and 25–30 minutes for well done. When cooked, remove from the oven, cover with foil and leave in a warm place for 10 minutes before carving. Arrange the lamb on a serving dish and serve with roasted root vegetables.

Get Ahead

To prepare ahead, complete the recipe to the end of step 4. Cool quickly and chill for up to 24 hours.
To use Bring the lamb to room temperature. Complete the recipe.

EASY		NUTRITIONAL INFORMATION		Serves
Preparation Time 30 minutes	**Cooking Time** 25–35 minutes, plus resting	**Per Serving** 488 calories, 39g fat (of which 15g saturates), 11g carbohydrate, 1.2g salt	Dairy free	**6**

Try Something Different

Use parsley instead of dill.

Marinated Rack of Lamb

500g (1lb 2oz) natural yogurt
large bunch of mint, chopped
large bunch of dill, chopped
3 garlic cloves, crushed
3 tbsp olive oil
2 trimmed racks of lamb
50g (2oz) fresh breadcrumbs
salt and ground black pepper

1 Put the yogurt, mint, dill, garlic and 2 tbsp oil in a shallow bowl, season and mix together. Transfer a quarter of the mixture to a small bowl, cover and chill.

2 Add the lamb to the remaining yogurt mixture and coat well. Cover and chill for at least 24 hours.

3 Preheat the oven to 200°C (180°C fan oven) mark 6. Put the lamb racks together so the ribs interlock and put in a roasting tin. Roast for 20–30 minutes. Remove from the tin, put on a board, cover with foil and leave to rest for 10 minutes.

4 Meanwhile, heat the remaining oil in a pan and fry the breadcrumbs until golden. Season with salt and sprinkle over the lamb. Serve immediately with the reserved yogurt dip.

Serves	EASY		NUTRITIONAL INFORMATION
6	**Preparation Time** 20 minutes, plus 24 hours marinating	**Cooking Time** 20–30 minutes, plus resting	**Per Serving** 406 calories, 31g fat (of which 14g saturates), 9g carbohydrate, 0.4g salt

Cook's Tip

Saffron Couscous: put 225g (8oz) couscous and 75g (3oz) raisins in a large bowl. Add a large pinch of saffron, ½ tsp salt and plenty of pepper. Pour 250ml (9fl oz) hot vegetable stock over, stir, cover and leave for 10 minutes to allow the couscous to swell and absorb the liquid. To serve, stir in 25g (1oz) toasted flaked almonds.

Moroccan Roasted Rack of Lamb

large bunch of fresh coriander

75g (3oz) pinenuts, fried in 1 tbsp olive oil

1 garlic clove, crushed

2 trimmed racks of lamb

2 tbsp harissa

salt and ground black pepper

Saffron Couscous (see Cook's Tip) to serve

1 Set aside 6 sprigs of coriander for the garnish and chop the rest roughly. Put the coriander, pinenuts and garlic in a mini food processor and blend to a coarse paste, or crush with a pestle and mortar.

2 Season the lamb and smear the curved side of each rack with the harissa. Press the pinenut and coriander mixture on top of the harissa. Cover and chill until needed.

3 Preheat the oven to 200°C (180°C fan oven) mark 6. Put the lamb in a roasting tin and roast for 20–25 minutes until the meat is just cooked and tender, yet slightly pink. Slice each rack into cutlets and serve with couscous, garnished with the reserved coriander.

EASY		NUTRITIONAL INFORMATION		Serves
Preparation Time 10 minutes	**Cooking Time** 30 minutes, plus resting	**Per Serving** 393 calories, 35g fat (of which 12g saturates), 1g carbohydrate, 0.2g salt	Dairy free	**6**

4

Beef

Classic Roast Beef with Yorkshire Puddings

1 boned and rolled rib, sirloin, rump or topside of beef, about 1.8kg (4lb)

1 tbsp plain flour

1 tbsp mustard powder

salt and ground black pepper

fresh thyme sprigs to garnish

vegetables to serve

For the gravy

150ml ($\frac{1}{4}$ pint) red wine

600ml (1 pint) beef stock

1 Preheat the oven to 230°C (210°C fan oven) mark 8. Put the beef in a roasting tin, with the thickest part of the fat uppermost. Mix the flour with the mustard powder, salt and pepper. Rub the mixture over the beef.

2 Roast the beef in the middle of the oven for 30 minutes.

3 Baste the beef and turn the oven down to 190°C (170°C fan oven) mark 5. Cook for a further 1 hour, approximately, basting occasionally. Meanwhile, prepare the Yorkshire pudding batter (see Cook's Tip).

4 Put the beef on a warmed carving dish, cover loosely with foil and leave to rest in a warm place. Increase the oven temperature to 220°C (200°C fan oven) mark 7 and cook the Yorkshire puddings.

5 Meanwhile, make the gravy. Skim off any remaining fat from the roasting tin. Put the tin on the hob, add the wine and boil until syrupy. Pour in the stock and, again, boil until syrupy; there should be about 450ml ($\frac{3}{4}$ pint) gravy. Taste and adjust the seasoning.

6 Carve the beef into slices. Garnish with thyme, serve with the gravy, Yorkshire puddings and vegetables of your choice.

Cook's Tip

Yorkshire Puddings: sift 125g (4oz) plain flour and $\frac{1}{2}$ tsp salt into a bowl. Mix in 150ml ($\frac{1}{4}$ pint) milk, then add 2 medium eggs, beaten, and season with pepper. Beat until smooth, then whisk in another 150ml ($\frac{1}{4}$ pint) milk. Pour about 3 tbsp fat from the beef roasting tin and use to grease 8–12 individual Yorkshire pudding tins. Put the tins in a preheated oven at 220°C (200°C fan oven) mark 7 for 5 minutes or until the fat is almost smoking. Pour the batter into the tins. Bake for 15–20 minutes until well risen, golden and crisp. Serve immediately.

Serves 8	EASY		NUTRITIONAL INFORMATION
	Preparation Time 20 minutes	**Cooking Time** about 1$\frac{1}{2}$ hours, plus resting	**Per Serving** 510 calories, 24g fat (of which 9g saturates), 16g carbohydrate, 0.5g salt

Beef Rib with Mustard, Parsley and Onion Crust

1 large onion, finely chopped

150ml (¼ pint) red wine or dry sherry

2.3kg (5lb) boned and rolled rib of beef

2 tbsp English mustard

2 tbsp freshly chopped flat-leafed parsley

salt and ground black pepper

roasted root vegetables and green vegetables to serve

1 Preheat the oven to 240°C (220°C fan oven) mark 9. Put the onion in a frying pan with the wine or sherry. Bring to the boil and bubble gently until most of the liquid has evaporated, then leave to cool.

2 Put the beef into a large roasting tin and season all over with pepper. Roast (with no extra fat) for 30 minutes. Turn the oven down to 190°C (170°C fan oven) mark 5 and continue to cook for 15 minutes per 450g (1lb) for rare, plus 15 minutes extra for medium-rare or 30 minutes extra for well-done meat.

3 About 10 minutes before the beef is cooked, transfer the joint to a smaller tin, keeping the large tin containing all the juices for the gravy. Smear the mustard all over the beef. Add the parsley to the cooled onion mixture, season with salt and pepper and press on to the beef. Put back in the oven to finish cooking.

4 Transfer the cooked beef to a warmed carving dish, cover loosely with foil and leave to rest for 30 minutes before serving. Carve the meat into slices and serve with roasted root vegetables and green vegetables.

Get Ahead

Cook the onion mixture (step 1), cool, cover and chill for up to 24 hours.

EASY		NUTRITIONAL INFORMATION		Serves
Preparation Time 20 minutes	**Cooking Time** about 2 hours, plus resting	**Per Serving** 501 calories, 26g fat (of which 10g saturates), 1.5g carbohydrate, 0.4g salt	Gluten free Dairy free	6

Mustard-roast Beef

1.1kg (2½lb) boned, rolled sirloin of beef

1 tbsp olive oil

5 bay leaves

200ml (7fl oz) red wine

2 onions, sliced

2 tbsp English mustard

300ml (½ pint) hot vegetable stock

salt and ground black pepper

1 Put the beef in a bowl and add the oil, bay leaves, wine and onions. Cover and marinate in the refrigerator for 4 hours or overnight.

2 Preheat the oven to 200°C (180°C fan oven) mark 6. Put the beef in a roasting tin with all the marinade ingredients. Spread the mustard over the meat, then season well with salt and pepper. Pour in the stock, then roast for 50–60 minutes. Cover and leave to rest for 10 minutes, then carve and serve.

Serves 4	EASY		NUTRITIONAL INFORMATION	
	Preparation Time 10 minutes	**Cooking Time** 50–60 minutes, plus resting	**Per Serving** 469 calories, 19g fat (of which 6g saturates), 3g carbohydrate, 0.5g salt	Gluten free Dairy free

Cook's Tip

Polenta: pour 900ml (1½ pints) milk into a large pan, add a pinch of salt and bring to the boil. Remove from the heat and add 150g (5oz) polenta in a slow stream, stirring constantly. Simmer, stirring, for 5 minutes. Remove from the heat and stir in 4 tbsp olive oil and 75g (3oz) finely grated Parmesan. Season with salt and pepper.

Fillet of Beef with Roquefort Sauce

125g (4oz) Roquefort cheese, crumbled
125g (4oz) unsalted butter, softened
900g (2lb) fillet of beef
7 tbsp vegetable oil
2 garlic cloves, crushed
2 large aubergines, 400g (14oz) each, cut lengthways into 1cm (½in) slices
150g (5oz) onion, finely chopped
150ml (¼ pint) medium-dry sherry
750ml (1¼ pints) beef stock
lemon juice to taste
salt and ground black pepper
polenta (see Cook's Tip) to serve

1 Gently stir the cheese into the butter. Cover and chill. Season the beef with salt and pepper. Heat 1 tbsp oil in a frying pan, add the beef and brown for 1–2 minutes on each side. Leave to cool.

2 Rub the beef with garlic. Brush each side of the aubergines with oil and fry in a non-stick frying pan for 4–5 minutes on each side until golden; cool. Wrap the aubergines around the beef and tie at intervals with string. Season and set aside.

3 Preheat the oven to 220°C (200°C fan oven) mark 7. Heat 2 tbsp oil in the frying pan and cook the onion for 10 minutes or until golden. Add the sherry, bring to the boil and bubble to reduce by half. Add the stock, bring to the boil again and bubble for 10–15 minutes until reduced by half. Set aside. Roast the beef for 30–40 minutes. Put the beef on a board, cover and leave to rest in a warm place for 10 minutes.

4 To make the sauce, reheat the sherry stock mixture, whisking in the Roquefort butter a little at a time. Add the lemon juice. Remove the string from the beef and slice. Stir any beef juices into the sauce. Serve the beef with the polenta and Roquefort sauce.

EASY		NUTRITIONAL INFORMATION		Serves
Preparation Time 30 minutes	**Cooking Time** about 1 hour 10 minutes, plus resting	**Per Serving** 610 calories, 46g fat (of which 2g saturates), 7g carbohydrate, 1.1g salt	Gluten free	**6**

Fillet of Beef with Horseradish and Walnut Cream

1 red onion, thinly sliced
2 tbsp olive oil
1.1kg (2½lb) fillet of beef
250ml (9fl oz) dry white wine
25g (1oz) walnut pieces
150ml (¼ pint) double cream
1 tbsp horseradish sauce
salt and ground black pepper
roast potatoes and green beans to serve

1 Preheat the oven to 220°C (200°C fan oven) mark 7. Put the onion into a flameproof roasting tin and drizzle 1 tbsp oil over it. Put the beef on top, season well and drizzle with the remaining oil. Roast for 15 minutes, carefully turning the beef once to brown it all over.

2 Turn the oven down to 170°C (150°C fan oven) mark 3, pour in the wine and continue roasting for another 25–30 minutes for rare, or 35–40 minutes for medium-rare. Put the beef on a board, cover with foil and leave to rest while you make the sauce.

3 Put the tin with the roasted onion and meat juices on the hob over a low heat. Add the walnuts, stir in the cream and horseradish and heat until bubbling. Cut the beef into thick slices and pour the horseradish and walnut cream over it. Serve with roast potatoes and green beans.

Serves	EASY		NUTRITIONAL INFORMATION	
6	**Preparation Time** 10 minutes	**Cooking Time** 45 minutes–1 hour, plus resting	**Per Serving** 449 calories, 27g fat (of which 13g saturates), 5g carbohydrate, 0.3g salt	Gluten free

1kg (2¼lb) fillet of beef, trimmed

100g (3½oz) butter

350ml (12fl oz) beef or veal stock

2 tbsp mixed peppercorns, crushed

1 tbsp vegetable oil

1 medium shallot, finely chopped

450g (1lb) mixed wild mushrooms, cleaned and trimmed

200g (7oz) cooked and peeled (or vacuum-packed) chestnuts, halved

3 tbsp finely chopped flat-leafed parsley

salt and ground black pepper

For the marinade

400ml (14fl oz) red wine

50ml (2fl oz) Madeira

2 tbsp balsamic vinegar

5 large shallots, sliced

1 bay leaf and 1 fresh thyme sprig

Fillet of Beef with Mushrooms and Chestnuts

1 Put the beef in a bowl, add the marinade ingredients, cover and leave in a cool place for 2–3 hours. Remove the shallots and beef with a slotted spoon; keep the liquid. Pat the beef dry with kitchen paper. Melt 25g (1oz) butter in a pan and gently fry the shallots. Add the marinade and boil until reduced to one-third. Add the stock and boil to reduce to one-third. Discard the bay and thyme. Set the sauce aside.

2 Preheat the oven to 200°C (180°C fan oven) mark 6. Roll the beef in the crushed peppercorns. Heat the oil in a heavy-based frying pan and brown the beef over a high heat. Put the beef in a roasting tin and roast for 25 minutes for medium-rare. Put the meat on a board, cover with foil and rest for 10 minutes.

3 Melt 25g (1oz) butter in a pan and cook the shallot until soft. Add the mushrooms and sauté until the liquid has evaporated. Stir in the chestnuts and parsley, and season. Set aside. Reheat the sauce and whisk in the remaining butter. Carve the beef and serve with the mushrooms, chestnuts and sauce.

EASY		NUTRITIONAL INFORMATION		Serves
				6
Preparation Time 20 minutes, plus 2–3 hours marinating	**Cooking Time** 45 minutes, plus resting	**Per Serving** 493 calories, 25g fat (of which 14g saturates), 16g carbohydrate, 0.5g salt	Gluten free	

Roast Beef with Tomato and Basil Sauce

800g (1lb 12oz) fillet of beef
2 tbsp olive oil
1 red onion, finely sliced
300g (11oz) cherry tomatoes, halved
1 tbsp red wine vinegar
100ml (3½fl oz) hot beef or vegetable stock
small handful of fresh basil leaves, roughly torn
salt and ground black pepper
new potatoes to serve

1 Preheat the oven to 200°C (180°C fan oven) mark 6. Season the beef with salt and pepper. Heat 1 tbsp oil in a large frying pan and fry the beef for 5 minutes, turning to brown on all sides. Put into a roasting tin and roast for 20–30 minutes – it should still be pink in the middle.

2 Meanwhile, pour the remaining oil into the pan in which you fried the beef. Add the onion and cook for 5–10 minutes over a medium heat until softened and golden. Add the tomatoes and continue to cook for 5 minutes until they're starting to soften.

3 Add the vinegar and stock and bring to the boil. Bubble for 1–2 minutes, then add the basil. Taste and adjust the seasoning.

4 Cover the meat with foil and leave to rest for 10 minutes. Carve into slices and serve with the sauce and new potatoes.

Serves 4	EASY		NUTRITIONAL INFORMATION	
	Preparation Time 10 minutes	**Cooking Time** about 35 minutes, plus resting	**Per Serving** 348 calories, 18g fat (of which 7g saturates), 4g carbohydrate, 0.2g salt	Gluten free Dairy free

1.4kg (3lb) topside or top rump of beef

1 tbsp balsamic vinegar

2 tbsp white wine vinegar

3 tbsp olive oil

3 tbsp freshly chopped marjoram or thyme

2 red peppers, cored, seeded and quartered

75g (3oz) fresh spinach, cooked and well drained

75g (3oz) pitted black olives, chopped

50g (2oz) smoked ham, chopped

75g (3oz) raisins or sultanas

salt and ground black pepper

roast potatoes and vegetables to serve

Stuffed Topside of Beef

1 Make a deep cut along the beef to create a pocket and put into a dish. Combine the vinegars, oil, marjoram or thyme and some pepper. Pour over the beef and into the pocket. Marinate in a cool place for 4–6 hours, or overnight.

2 Grill the peppers, skin-side up, under a hot grill until the skins are charred. Cool in a covered bowl, then remove the skins.

3 Squeeze excess water from the spinach, then chop and put into a bowl with the olives, ham and raisins. Mix well and season with salt and pepper.

4 Preheat the oven to 190°C (170°C fan oven) mark 5. Line the pocket of the beef with the peppers, keeping back two pepper quarters for the gravy. Spoon the spinach mixture into the pocket and spread evenly. Reshape the meat and tie at intervals with string.

5 Put the beef into a roasting tin just large enough to hold it. Pour the marinade over it and roast for 1 hour for rare beef, or 1¼ hours for medium-rare, basting from time to time. Put the beef on a board, cover with foil and leave to rest in a warm place while you make the gravy.

6 Skim off the excess fat from the roasting tin. Put the tin on the hob and bring the pan juices to the boil. Add 125ml (4fl oz) water and bubble for 2–3 minutes. Finely chop the remaining pepper pieces and add to the gravy.

7 Carve the beef and serve with the gravy, roast potatoes and vegetables of your choice.

EASY		NUTRITIONAL INFORMATION		Serves
Preparation Time 35 minutes, plus marinating	**Cooking Time** 1–1¼ hours, plus resting	**Per Serving** 535 calories, 29g fat (of which 10g saturates), 13g carbohydrate, 1.4g salt	Gluten free Dairy free	**6**

Cook's Tip

Red Wine Sauce: soften 350g (12oz) shallots, finely
chopped, in 2 tbsp olive oil for 5 minutes. Add 3 garlic
cloves, chopped, and 3 tbsp tomato purée, cook for
1 minute, then add 2 tbsp balsamic vinegar. Simmer briskly
until reduced to almost nothing, then add 200ml (7fl oz)
red wine and reduce by half. Pour in 600ml (1 pint) beef
stock and simmer until reduced by one-third.

Fillet of Beef en Croûte

1–1.4kg (2¼–3lb) fillet of beef, trimmed

50g (2oz) butter

2 shallots, chopped

15g (½oz) dried porcini mushrooms, soaked in 100ml
(3½fl oz) boiling water

2 garlic cloves, chopped

225g (8oz) flat mushrooms, finely chopped

2 tsp chopped fresh thyme, plus extra sprigs to garnish

175g (6oz) chicken liver pâté

175g (6oz) thinly sliced Parma ham

375g ready-rolled puff pastry

1 medium egg, beaten

salt and ground black pepper

Red Wine Sauce (see Cook's Tip) to serve

1 Season the beef with salt and pepper. Melt 25g (1oz)
butter in a large frying pan and, when foaming, add
the beef and cook for 4–5 minutes to brown all over.
Transfer to a plate and leave to cool.

2 Melt the remaining butter in a pan, add the shallots
and cook for 1 minute. Drain the porcini mushrooms,
reserving the liquid, and chop them. Add them to the
pan with the garlic, the reserved liquid and the fresh
mushrooms. Turn up the heat and cook until the
liquid has evaporated, then season with salt and
pepper and add the thyme. Leave to cool.

3 Put the chicken liver pâté in a bowl and beat until
smooth. Add the mushroom mixture and stir well.
Spread half the mushroom mixture evenly over one
side of the fillet. Lay half the Parma ham on a length
of clingfilm, overlapping the slices. Invert the
mushroom-topped beef on to the ham. Spread the
remaining mushroom mixture on the other side of
the beef, then lay the rest of the Parma ham, also
overlapping, on top of the mushroom mixture. Wrap
the beef in the clingfilm to form a firm sausage
shape, and chill for 30 minutes. Preheat the oven to
220°C (200°C fan oven) mark 7.

4 Cut off one-third of the pastry and roll out on a
lightly floured surface to 3mm (⅛in) thick and
2.5cm (1in) larger all round than the beef. Prick
all over with a fork. Transfer to a baking sheet
and bake for 12–15 minutes until brown and crisp.
Leave to cool, then trim to the size of the beef
and place on a baking sheet. Remove the clingfilm
from the beef, brush with the egg and place on the
cooked pastry.

5 Roll out the remaining pastry to a 25.5 x 30.5cm
(10 x 12in) rectangle. Roll over a lattice pastry cutter
and gently ease the lattice open. Cover the beef with
the lattice, tuck the ends under and seal the edges.
Brush with the beaten egg, then cook for 40 minutes
for rare to medium, 45 minutes for medium. Leave to
rest for 10 minutes before carving. Garnish with
thyme and serve with Red Wine Sauce.

FOR THE CONFIDENT COOK		NUTRITIONAL INFORMATION	Serves
Preparation Time 1 hour, plus soaking and chilling	**Cooking Time** about 1 hour 20 minutes, plus resting	**Per Serving** 802 calories, 53g fat (of which 15g saturates), 27g carbohydrate, 2.4g salt	**6**

Roast Rib of Beef

2-bone rib of beef, about 2.5-2.7kg (5½-6lb)

1 tbsp plain flour

1 tbsp mustard powder

150ml (5fl oz) red wine

600ml (1 pint) beef stock

600ml (1 pint) water from parboiled potatoes

salt and ground black pepper

Yorkshire puddings, roasted root vegetables and a green vegetable to serve

1 Preheat the oven to 230°C (210°C fan oven) mark 8. Put the beef, fat-side up, in a roasting tin just large enough to hold the joint. Mix the flour and mustard together in a small bowl and season with salt and pepper, then rub the mixture over the beef. Roast in the centre of the oven for 30 minutes.

2 Move the beef to a lower shelf, near the bottom of the oven. Turn the oven down to 220°C (200°C fan oven) mark 7 and continue to roast for a further 2 hours, basting occasionally.

3 Put the beef on a carving dish, cover loosely with foil and leave to rest while you make the gravy. Skim off most of the fat from the roasting tin. Put the roasting tin on the hob, pour in the wine and boil vigorously until very syrupy. Pour in the stock and boil until syrupy. Add the vegetable water and boil until syrupy. There should be about 450ml (¾ pint) gravy. Taste and adjust the seasoning.

4 Remove the rib bone and carve the beef. Serve with gravy, Yorkshire puddings and vegetables.

Serves	EASY		NUTRITIONAL INFORMATION
8	**Preparation Time** 5 minutes	**Cooking Time** 2½ hours, plus resting	**Per Serving** 807 calories, 53g fat (of which 24g saturates), 2g carbohydrate, 0.5g salt

Cook's Tips

If any anchovy mixture falls off the beef, whisk it into the gravy.

Anchovies are salty, so don't add too much salt.

Beef with Tapenade

50g can anchovy fillets, drained

2 tbsp capers and 2 garlic cloves

1 tbsp Dijon mustard

4 tbsp freshly chopped flat-leaf parsley and about 15 fresh mint leaves

1 tbsp balsamic vinegar

3 tbsp extra virgin olive oil

900g (2lb) rolled topside of beef

1 tbsp plain flour

600ml (1 pint) beef stock

150ml (¼ pint) red wine

salt and ground black pepper

polenta (see page 89), mashed potatoes or roast potatoes and green vegetables to serve

1 Whiz the anchovies in a food processor with the capers, garlic, mustard, herbs and vinegar. With the motor running, add 1 tbsp oil and blend to combine.

2 Untie the topside, trim away any excess fat and season the meat with salt and pepper. Make a deep cut along the beef to create a pocket. Spread half the anchovy mixture inside the cut. Fold the meat back over and tie at intervals with string. Preheat the oven to 220°C (200°C fan oven) mark 7.

3 Heat the remaining oil in a flameproof roasting tin and brown the meat well on all sides. Cook in the oven for 25 minutes for rare; 30 minutes for medium; 35–40 minutes for well-done. Spread a little of the remaining anchovy mixture over the meat and put back in the oven for 5–10 minutes. Put the meat on a carving dish, cover and leave to rest for 10–15 minutes.

4 Put the roasting tin on the hob, stir the flour into the juices and cook over a low heat for 1 minute, stirring. Gradually whisk in the stock and wine, bring to the boil and bubble for 10 minutes or until reduced by half. Slice the beef and serve with the sauce, polenta – or roast potatoes – and vegetables.

Serves 4	EASY		NUTRITIONAL INFORMATION	
	Preparation Time 15 minutes	**Cooking Time** 35–50 minutes, plus resting	**Per Serving** 534 calories, 31g fat (of which 10g saturates), 3g carbohydrate, 1.6g salt	Dairy free

Cook's Tip

This is equally good hot – with roast potatoes, carrots and green cabbage – or cold, with salad, mustardy mayonnaise, gherkins and bread.

1.8kg (4lb) piece boned, salted silverside

1 onion, sliced

4 carrots, sliced

1 small turnip, sliced

1–2 celery sticks, chopped

8 cloves

125g (4oz) light muscovado sugar

½ tsp mustard powder

1 tsp ground cinnamon

juice of 1 orange

Spiced Silverside

1 Soak the meat for several hours or overnight in enough cold water to cover it.

2 Rinse the meat and put into a large, heavy-based pan with the vegetables. Add water to cover the meat and bring slowly to the boil. Skim off any scum, cover with a lid and simmer for 4 hours. Leave to cool in the liquid.

3 Drain the meat well, then put into a roasting tin and press the cloves into the fat. Mix together the sugar, mustard, cinnamon and orange juice and spread over the meat. Preheat the oven to 180°C (160°C fan oven) mark 4.

4 Roast for 45 minutes to 1 hour, basting from time to time. Serve hot or cold (see Cook's Tip).

EASY		NUTRITIONAL INFORMATION		Serves
Preparation Time 20 minutes, plus soaking	**Cooking Time** 4–5 hours	**Per Serving** 339 calories, 8g fat (of which 3g saturates), 28g carbohydrate, 4.2g salt	Gluten free Dairy free	**6**

5

Vegetables

Freezing Tip

To freeze Complete the recipe to step 3, cool, cover and freeze for up to one month.

To use Cook from frozen for 45 minutes, then unwrap the foil slightly and cook for a further 15 minutes until turning golden.

White Nut Roast

40g (1½oz) butter

1 onion, finely chopped

1 garlic clove, crushed

225g (8oz) mixed white nuts, such as brazils, macadamias, pinenuts and whole almonds, ground in a food processor

125g (4oz) fresh white breadcrumbs

grated zest and juice of ½ lemon

75g (3oz) sage Derby cheese or Parmesan, grated

125g (4oz) cooked, peeled (or vacuum-packed) chestnuts, roughly chopped

½ x 400g can artichoke hearts, roughly chopped

1 medium egg, lightly beaten

2 tsp each freshly chopped parsley, sage and thyme, plus extra sprigs

salt and ground black pepper

1 Preheat the oven to 200°C (180°C fan oven) mark 6. Melt the butter in a pan and cook the onion and garlic for 5 minutes or until soft. Put into a large bowl and set aside to cool.

2 Add the nuts, breadcrumbs, zest and juice of the lemon, cheese, chestnuts and artichokes. Season well and bind together with the egg. Stir in the herbs.

3 Put the mixture on to a large piece of buttered foil and shape into a fat sausage, packing tightly. Scatter with the extra herb sprigs and wrap in the foil.

4 Cook on a baking sheet for 35 minutes, then unwrap the foil slightly and cook for a further 15 minutes until turning golden.

Serves 8	EASY		NUTRITIONAL INFORMATION	
	Preparation Time 20 minutes	**Cooking Time** about 1 hour	**Per Serving** 371 calories, 28g fat (of which 9g saturates), 20g carbohydrate, 0.8g salt	Vegetarian

Try Something Different

Leave out the celery. Add 50g (2oz) pitted black olives, chopped, to the bulgur wheat mixture and use feta cheese instead of the goat's cheese.

4 large red peppers, halved and seeded

2 tbsp olive oil

100g (3½oz) bulgur wheat

1 red onion, finely chopped

1 tsp ground coriander

2 celery sticks, finely chopped

2 courgettes, finely chopped

200g (7oz) chestnut mushrooms, finely chopped

25g (1oz) pinenuts

100g (3½oz) goat's cheese, roughly chopped

salt and ground black pepper

Stuffed Peppers

1 Preheat the oven to 200°C (180°C fan oven) mark 6. Put the peppers in a roasting tin, brush with 1 tbsp oil and roast for 20 minutes. Put the bulgur wheat in a pan and cook according to the packet instructions.

2 Meanwhile, heat the remaining oil in a frying pan. Fry the onion for 5–7 minutes until soft. Add the coriander and fry for a further minute. Add the celery, courgettes and mushrooms and cook for 10 minutes. Tip into a bowl.

3 Add the cooked bulgur wheat, pinenuts and goat's cheese to the onion mixture, season well and mix thoroughly. Spoon the mixture into the pepper halves and put back in the oven to heat through.

EASY		NUTRITIONAL INFORMATION		Serves
Preparation Time 20 minutes	**Cooking Time** 35–45 minutes	**Per Serving** 351 calories, 18g fat (of which 6g saturates), 35g carbohydrate, 0.4g salt	Vegetarian	**4**

Red Cabbage Timbales with Mushroom Stuffing

1 medium red cabbage, about 1.4kg (3lb)

Mushroom and Cashew Nut Stuffing (see Cook's Tip)

40g (1^1/$_2$oz) butter

375g (12oz) onions, finely chopped

3 tbsp balsamic vinegar

salt and ground black pepper

small thyme sprigs to garnish (optional)

green vegetables to serve

For the sauce

4 tbsp caster sugar

4 tbsp red wine vinegar

150ml (^{1}/$_4$ pint) red wine

1 tbsp lemon juice

Cook's Tip

- -

Mushroom and Cashew Nut Stuffing: melt 50g (2oz) butter in a pan, add 200g (7oz) onions, finely chopped, and cook until soft and golden. Add 450g (1lb) chestnut mushrooms, roughly chopped, and fry over a moderate heat or until the moisture has evaporated. Stir in 75g (3oz) roughly chopped salted cashew nuts, 4 tbsp freshly chopped flat-leafed parsley and 125g (4oz) fresh breadcrumbs. Leave to cool, then stir in 2 large eggs, beaten, and season with salt and pepper. Mix well, then cover and set aside. This stuffing can also be used for chicken or turkey.

1 Put the cabbage in a large pan of boiling water. Bring to the boil; simmer until the outside leaves have softened enough to be eased away. Lift the cabbage out of the pan; keep the water. Remove three outer leaves and boil them for a further 3–4 minutes; place in a bowl of cold water. Quarter the whole cabbage and remove the core. Take 700g (1^1/$_2$lb) of the cabbage, remove and discard any thick central vein, then shred the leaves very finely, cover and set aside. Preheat the oven to 190°C (170°C fan oven) mark 5. Line six 150ml (^{1}/$_4$ pint) moulds with clingfilm. Drain the whole cabbage leaves and cut in half; discard the central vein. Use the leaves to line the moulds. Fill with stuffing and cover with foil. Place in a large roasting tin; pour in enough warm water to come halfway up the sides of the moulds. Cook for 30 minutes or until just set to the centre.

2 Meanwhile, melt the butter in a pan, add the onions and cook until soft. Mix in the shredded cabbage, vinegar, 3 tbsp water and season. Cook, stirring from time to time, for 15–20 minutes until just tender.

3 To make the sauce, put the sugar and vinegar in a small pan. Cook over a low heat until the sugar has dissolved, then bring to the boil and cook to a rich caramel. Pour in the wine, allow to reduce by half, add lemon juice to taste and season. Cool.

4 Turn out the timbales, spoon shredded cabbage on top and around, drizzle the sauce over and garnish with thyme, if you like. Serve with green vegetables.

A LITTLE EFFORT		NUTRITIONAL INFORMATION		Serves
Preparation Time 1 hour, plus cooling	**Cooking Time** 1 hour	**Per Serving** 454 calories, 22g fat (of which 10g saturates), 49g carbohydrate, 0.8g salt	Vegetarian	**6**

1 pumpkin, about 1.4–1.8kg (3–4lb)

2 tbsp olive oil

2 leeks, trimmed and chopped

2 garlic cloves, crushed

2 tbsp freshly chopped thyme leaves

2 tsp paprika

1 tsp turmeric

125g (4oz) long-grain rice, cooked

2 tomatoes, peeled, seeded and diced

50g (2oz) cashew nuts, toasted and roughly chopped

125g (4oz) Cheddar cheese, grated

salt and ground black pepper

Baked Stuffed Pumpkin

1 Cut a 5cm (2in) slice from the top of the pumpkin and set aside for the lid. Scoop out and discard the seeds. Using a knife and a spoon, cut out most of the pumpkin flesh, leaving a thin shell. Cut the pumpkin flesh into small pieces and set aside.

2 Heat the oil in a large pan, add the leeks, garlic, thyme, paprika and turmeric, and fry for 10 minutes. Add the chopped pumpkin flesh and fry for a further 10 minutes until golden, stirring frequently to prevent sticking. Transfer the mixture to a bowl. Preheat the oven to 180°C (160°C fan oven) mark 4.

3 Add the pumpkin mixture to the cooked rice along with the tomatoes, cashews and cheese. Fork through to mix and season with salt and pepper.

4 Spoon the stuffing mixture into the pumpkin shell, top with the lid and bake for 1¼–1½ hours until the pumpkin is softened and the skin is browned. Remove from the oven and leave to stand for 10 minutes. Cut into wedges to serve.

Serves 4	EASY		NUTRITIONAL INFORMATION	
	Preparation Time about 40 minutes	**Cooking Time** 1½ hours–1 hour 50 minutes, plus standing	**Per Serving** 438 calories, 24g fat (of which 9g saturates), 38g carbohydrate, 0.7g salt	Vegetarian Gluten free

Sweet Roasted Fennel

700g (1½lb) fennel (about 3 bulbs)

3 tbsp olive oil

50g (2oz) butter, melted

1 lemon, halved

1 tsp caster sugar

2 large thyme sprigs

salt and ground black pepper

1 Preheat the oven to 200°C (180°C fan oven) mark 6. Trim and quarter the fennel and put in a large roasting tin.

2 Drizzle the fennel with the oil and melted butter and squeeze over the lemon juice. Add the lemon halves to the roasting tin. Sprinkle with sugar and season generously with salt and pepper. Add the thyme and cover with a damp piece of non-stick baking parchment.

3 Roast for 30 minutes then remove the baking parchment and cook for a further 20–30 minutes until lightly charred and tender.

EASY		NUTRITIONAL INFORMATION		
Preparation Time 10 minutes	**Cooking Time** about 1 hour	**Per Serving** 192 calories, 19g fat (of which 8g saturates), 4g carbohydrate, 0.2g salt	Vegetarian Gluten free	Serves **4**

Cook's Tips

To make a nutritionally complete meal, sprinkle with toasted sesame seeds and serve with hummus.
Use oregano instead of thyme.

Roasted Mediterranean Vegetables

4 plum tomatoes, halved
2 onions, peeled and quartered
4 red peppers, seeded and cut into strips
2 courgettes, cut into thick slices
4 garlic cloves, unpeeled
6 tbsp olive oil
1 tbsp freshly chopped thyme leaves
sea salt flakes and ground black pepper

1 Preheat the oven to 220°C (200°C fan oven) mark 7. Put the tomatoes in a large roasting tin with the onions, peppers, courgettes and garlic. Drizzle with the oil and sprinkle with thyme, sea salt flakes and black pepper.

2 Roast, turning occasionally, for 35–40 minutes until tender.

Serves	EASY		NUTRITIONAL INFORMATION	
4	**Preparation Time** 10 minutes	**Cooking Time** 35–40 minutes	**Per Serving** 252 calories, 18g fat (of which 3g saturates), 19g carbohydrate, 0.4g salt	Vegetarian Gluten free • Dairy free

Try Something Different

Use crushed garlic instead of chilli.

Roasted Butternut Squash

2 butternut squash

2 tbsp olive oil

25g (1oz) butter

2 tbsp freshly chopped thyme leaves

1 red chilli, seeded and finely chopped (see page 69)

salt and ground black pepper

1 Preheat the oven to 220°C (200°C fan oven) mark 7. Cut the squash in half lengthways and scoop out the seeds. Cut in half again, then put into a roasting tin. Drizzle with the oil, season with salt and pepper and roast for 40 minutes.

2 Meanwhile, put the butter into a bowl with the thyme and chilli. Mix together well. Add a little to each slice of cooked butternut squash.

EASY		NUTRITIONAL INFORMATION		Serves
Preparation Time 15 minutes	**Cooking Time** 40 minutes	**Per Serving** 165 calories, 12g fat (of which 5g saturates), 11g carbohydrate, 0.1g salt	Vegetarian Gluten free	**4**

Sage-roasted Parsnips, Apples and Prunes

6–8 tbsp olive oil

1.8kg (4lb) parsnips, peeled, quartered and cored

6 apples, peeled, cored and quartered

16 ready-to-eat prunes

50g (2oz) butter

1–2 tbsp freshly chopped sage leaves

1–2 tbsp clear honey (optional)

salt and ground black pepper

1 Heat 3–4 tbsp oil in a large flameproof roasting tin, add the parsnips in batches and fry over a medium heat until a rich golden brown all over. Remove from the tin and set aside. Add 3–4 tbsp oil to the same tin. Fry the apples until golden brown. Remove from the tin and set aside.

2 Preheat the oven to 200°C (180°C fan oven) mark 6. Put the parsnips back in the tin, season with salt and pepper and roast for 15 minutes.

3 Add the apples and continue roasting for 10 minutes. Put the prunes in the tin and roast for a further 5 minutes. At the end of this time, test the apples. If they're still firm, roast everything for a further 5–10 minutes until the apples are soft and fluffy.

4 Put the tin on the hob over a very low heat. Add the butter and sage, drizzle with honey if you like, and spoon into a hot serving dish.

Get Ahead

Fry the parsnips and apples, then cool, cover and chill for up to one day.

Serves	EASY		NUTRITIONAL INFORMATION	
8	**Preparation Time** 20 minutes	**Cooking Time** 45–55 minutes	**Per Serving** 313 calories, 16g fat (of which 5g saturates), 40g carbohydrate, 0.2g salt	Vegetarian Gluten free

Mustard-roasted Potatoes and Parsnips

1.4kg (3lb) small, even-sized potatoes, scrubbed
800g (1lb 12oz) small parsnips, peeled
50g (2oz) goose fat
1–2 tbsp black mustard seeds
1 tbsp sea salt

1 Cut out small wedges from one side of each of the potatoes and parsnips (this will help make them extra crispy). Put them into a pan of salted cold water, bring to the boil and cook for 6 minutes. Drain well.

2 Preheat the oven to 200°C (180°C fan oven) mark 6. Heat the goose fat in a roasting tin for 4–5 minutes until sizzling hot. Add the potatoes, toss in the fat and roast for 30 minutes. Add the parsnips and sprinkle with the mustard seeds and sea salt. Roast for a further 30–35 minutes, turning after 20 minutes, until the vegetables are golden.

Serves	EASY		NUTRITIONAL INFORMATION	
8	**Preparation Time** 25 minutes	**Cooking Time** about 1 hour	**Per Serving** 251 calories, 8g fat (of which 3g saturates), 43g carbohydrate, 1.9g salt	Gluten free Dairy free

Roasted Parma Potatoes

about 50 fresh sage leaves

900g (2lb) new potatoes (around 25), scrubbed

200g (7oz) thinly sliced Parma ham, torn into strips

4 tbsp olive oil

salt and ground black pepper

1 Preheat the oven to 200°C (180°C fan oven) mark 6. Put two sage leaves on each potato and wrap a strip of Parma ham around. Repeat until all the potatoes are wrapped.

2 Put half the oil in an ovenproof dish. Add the potatoes, drizzle with the remaining oil and season well. Roast for 45–50 minutes until tender.

EASY		NUTRITIONAL INFORMATION		Serves
Preparation Time 25 minutes	**Cooking Time** 45–50 minutes	**Per Serving** 201 calories, 9g fat (of which 2g saturates), 24g carbohydrate, 0.9g salt	Gluten free Dairy free	**4**

Freezing Tip

To freeze Complete step 1. Spread out the potatoes on a baking tray and leave to cool, then freeze on the tray. Once frozen, put them into a plastic bag and freeze for up to three months.
To use Roast from frozen, following step 2, for 1 hour 20 minutes–1¹/₂ hours.

Saffron-roasted Potatoes

1.4kg (3lb) small, even-sized potatoes, peeled

2 large pinches of saffron threads

4 tbsp goose fat

2 tbsp coarse sea salt

1 Put the potatoes in a pan of salted cold water, add the saffron, cover, bring to the boil and cook for 6 minutes. Drain and shake in a colander to roughen the surface of the potatoes.

2 Preheat the oven to 200°C (180°C fan oven) mark 6. Heat the fat in a roasting tin for 4–5 minutes. Add the potatoes, sprinkle with salt and roast for 1 hour until golden, shaking the pan after 30 minutes.

Serves 8	EASY		NUTRITIONAL INFORMATION	
	Preparation Time 15 minutes	**Cooking Time** about 1 hour	**Per Serving** 198 calories, 8g fat (of which 3g saturates), 30g carbohydrate, 0.1g salt	Gluten free Dairy free

Try Something Different

Use other combinations of vegetables: try celeriac instead of parsnips, fennel instead of swede, peeled shallots instead of carrots.

Roasted Root Vegetables

1 large potato, cut into large chunks
1 large sweet potato, cut into large chunks
3 carrots, cut into large chunks
4 small parsnips, halved
1 small swede, cut into large chunks
3 tbsp olive oil
2 fresh rosemary and 2 fresh thyme sprigs
salt and ground black pepper

1 Preheat the oven to 200°C (180°C fan oven) mark 6. Put all the vegetables into a large roasting tin. Add the oil.

2 Use scissors to snip the herbs over the vegetables, then season with salt and pepper and toss everything together. Roast for 1 hour or until tender.

EASY		NUTRITIONAL INFORMATION		Serves
Preparation Time 15 minutes	**Cooking Time** 1 hour	**Per Serving** 251 calories, 10g fat (of which 1g saturates), 39g carbohydrate, 0.2g salt	Vegetarian Gluten free • Dairy free	**4**

6

Sauces and Gravies

Try Something Different

- -

Add 1-2 tbsp dry sherry after adding the stock; it will add a subtle flavour and the alcohol will cook off as the gravy bubbles.

Perfect Gravy

juices in the roasting tin

about 2 tbsp plain flour

about 1.1 litres (2 pints) stock (see pages 22-23)

salt and ground black pepper

1 Make the gravy while the meat or poultry is resting. Tilt the roasting tin to tip the liquid into one corner. Spoon off most of the fat, leaving about 2 tbsp fat and the juices in the tin.

2 Put the roasting tin on the hob over a low heat and add the flour. Stir it in with a wooden spoon and cook for 1-2 minutes. Don't worry if it looks horribly lumpy at this point.

3 Gradually pour in the stock, whisking it in using a balloon whisk. Bring the gravy to the boil, whisking all the time, then let it bubble and reduce a little to concentrate the flavour. Taste, season and keep warm until ready to serve.

Serves 8	EASY		NUTRITIONAL INFORMATION	
	Preparation Time 2 minutes	**Cooking Time** 8 minutes	**Per Serving** 45 calories, 3g fat (of which 1g saturates), 4g carbohydrate, 0.2g salt	Dairy free

Mushroom and White Wine Gravy

20g (³/₄oz) dried chanterelle mushrooms, chopped
25g (1oz) butter
1 tbsp olive oil
75g (3oz) shallots, finely sliced
300ml (½ pint) dry white wine
250ml (9fl oz) stock (see pages 22–23)
juices in the roasting tin
200ml (7fl oz) crème fraîche (optional)
salt and ground black pepper

1 Rinse the mushrooms. Put in a bowl and add 300ml (½ pint) boiling water. Leave to soak for 30 minutes.

2 Gently heat the butter and oil together in a pan, then sauté the shallots for 5 minutes or until soft.

3 Add the wine and boil to reduce by at least half. Meanwhile, strain the mushrooms, reserving the soaking water. Add the stock, soaking water and the soaked mushrooms, then simmer for 5 minutes.

4 While the meat or poultry is resting, skim the fat from the roasting tin and discard, then add the juices to the gravy. Add the crème fraîche if using, and heat through. Season with salt and pepper.

EASY		NUTRITIONAL INFORMATION		Serves
Preparation Time 15 minutes, plus 30 minutes soaking	**Cooking Time** 15 minutes	**Per Serving** 78 calories, 6g fat (of which 3g saturates), 1g carbohydrate, 0.3g salt	Gluten free	**8**

Try Something Different

Instead of redcurrant jelly use tomato purée for a more
savoury flavour.
Red Wine Gravy: instead of Madeira use red wine and
instead of redcurrant jelly use fine shred marmalade.

Rich Madeira Gravy

juices in the roasting tin
40g (1½oz) plain flour
150ml (¼ pint) Madeira
about 1.1 litres (2 pints) stock (see pages 22–23)
2 tbsp redcurrant jelly
salt and ground black pepper

1 While the meat or poultry is resting, pour off as
much of the fat as you can from the roasting tin,
leaving just the dark brown juices. Put the roasting
tin on the hob over a low heat, stir in the flour with
a wooden spoon, then gradually pour in the Madeira
and bubble for 1 minute.

2 Gradually pour in the stock and mix in, scraping up
all the goodness from the base of the tin. Bring to
the boil, then add the redcurrant jelly and simmer for
5 minutes. Season, then pour through a sieve into a
sauce boat and keep warm until ready to serve.

Serves 8	EASY		NUTRITIONAL INFORMATION	
	Preparation Time 2 minutes	**Cooking Time** about 10 minutes	**Per Serving** 80 calories, 3g fat (of which 1g saturates), 8g carbohydrate, 0.2g salt	Dairy free

Freezing Tip

To freeze Tip into a freezerproof container and cool, then label and freeze for up to one month.
To use Thaw and serve warm or cold.

Cranberry Sauce

225g (8oz) fresh cranberries
grated zest and juice of 1 orange
4 tbsp fine shred marmalade
125g (4oz) light muscovado sugar
50ml (2fl oz) port

1 Put the cranberries into a pan. Add the orange zest and juice, marmalade, sugar and port. Mix together well, then bring to the boil and simmer for 5–10 minutes, stirring occasionally, until thickened.

EASY		NUTRITIONAL INFORMATION		Serves
Preparation Time 10 minutes	**Cooking Time** about 10 minutes	**Per Serving** 101 calories, trace fat, 25g carbohydrate, 0g salt	Vegetarian Gluten free • Dairy free	**8**

Freezing Tip

To freeze Complete the recipe, tip into a freezerproof container and cool. Label and freeze for up to one month. **To use** Thaw, reheat gently with an extra 2 tbsp cream, then simmer for 2 minutes until piping hot.

Bread Sauce

1 onion, peeled and quartered
4 cloves
2 bay leaves
600ml (1 pint) milk
125g (4oz) fresh white breadcrumbs
4 tbsp double cream
25g (1oz) butter
a little freshly grated nutmeg
salt and ground black pepper

1 Stud each onion quarter with a clove, then put into a pan with the bay leaves and milk. Bring to the boil, take off the heat and leave to infuse for 10 minutes.

2 Use a slotted spoon to lift out the onion and bay leaves; discard. Add the breadcrumbs to the pan and bring to the boil, stirring. Simmer for 5–6 minutes.

3 Stir in the cream and butter, then add the nutmeg and season with salt and pepper. Spoon into a warmed serving dish.

Serves 8	EASY		NUTRITIONAL INFORMATION	
	Preparation Time 15 minutes, plus 10 minutes standing	**Cooking Time** about 20 minutes	**Per Serving** 150 calories, 8g fat (of which 5g saturates), 16g carbohydrate, 0.4g salt	Vegetarian

Cook's Tip

This sauce is perfect with roast lamb and works just as well with turkey.

Redcurrant Sauce

600ml (1 pint) fruity red wine

6 tbsp redcurrant jelly

3 tbsp Worcestershire sauce

juice of 1 lemon

juice of 1 orange

juices in the roasting tin

2 tbsp plain flour

2 tsp English mustard powder

1 Pour the wine into a small pan and add the redcurrant jelly, Worcestershire sauce and the lemon and orange juices. Heat very gently until the jelly melts.

2 Pour off all but 2 tbsp fat from the roasting tin. Put the tin on the hob over a low heat and stir in the flour and mustard powder to make a paste.

3 Increase the heat and pour in the wine mixture, a little at a time. Mix with a wooden spoon after each addition, scraping up any crusty bits from the bottom of the tin. Once all the wine has been incorporated, swap the spoon for a whisk and whisk until the sauce is smooth. Reduce the heat and bubble gently for 10 minutes, then pour into a warm jug to serve.

EASY		NUTRITIONAL INFORMATION		Serves
Preparation Time 10 minutes	**Cooking Time** 25 minutes	**Per Serving** 118 calories, 3g fat (of which 1g saturates), 9g carbohydrate, 0.4g salt	Dairy free	**8**

Freezing Tip

To freeze Complete the recipe, cool and freeze for up to one month.
To use Thaw at cool room temperature. Put in a pan, add 2–3 tbsp milk and slowly bring to the boil. Simmer over a medium heat for 2–3 minutes. Add a little more milk if the sauce is too thick.

Onion Sauce

600ml (1 pint) milk
2 large onions
10 peppercorns
1 large mace blade
1 large bay leaf
40g (1½oz) butter
40g (1½oz) plain flour
freshly grated nutmeg
salt and ground black pepper

1 Pour the milk into a pan. Halve the onions, cut two thin slices off one half and add them to the milk; set the rest aside. Add the peppercorns, mace and bay leaf, bring almost to the boil, then remove from the heat, cover and leave to infuse for about 20 minutes. Strain.

2 Meanwhile, finely dice the remaining onion and sauté in 15g (½oz) butter for 10-15 minutes until softened.

3 Melt the remaining butter in a separate pan, stir in the flour and cook, stirring constantly, for 1 minute until cooked but not coloured. Remove from the heat and gradually pour in the milk, whisking constantly. Season with nutmeg, salt and pepper.

4 Add the softened onion, return to the heat and cook, stirring, until the sauce is thickened and smooth; simmer gently for 2 minutes. Serve warm, with roast goose.

Serves 8	EASY		NUTRITIONAL INFORMATION	
	Preparation Time 5 minutes, plus infusing	Cooking Time about 20 minutes	Per Serving 303 calories, 23g fat (of which 14g saturates), 22g carbohydrate, 0.3g salt	Vegetarian